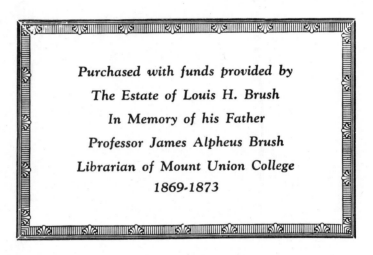

# EXTRAORDINARY CHILDREN

## ORDINARY LIVES

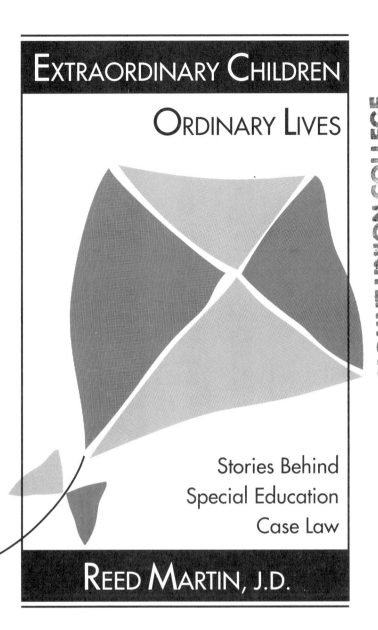

Stories Behind
Special Education
Case Law

# REED MARTIN, J.D.

RESEARCH PRESS • 2612 NORTH MATTIS AVENUE • CHAMPAIGN, IL 61821

Cover design by Elizabeth D. Burczy, Chicago, Illinois
Composition by Wadley Graphix Corporation
Printed by McNaughton & Gunn

ISBN 0-87822-332-0
Library of Congress Catalog No. 91-62230

3-4-1.0791
M382e

251228

On the day the United States Senate passed the Education for All Handicapped Children Act, Senator Robert Stafford of Vermont said:

*This thing that we do, then, is not only an act of law for equality in education, but an act of love for those extraordinary children wishing only to live ordinary lives.*

This book is dedicated to all the extraordinary children who let me be a part of their struggle for an ordinary life.

# Contents

# Acknowledgments

The first case described in this book, *Jill*, is the only one on which I worked alone. Dozens of other lawyers worked on the remaining cases. Working even harder were the parents involved: Joan, Judy, Elaine, Mary, Carmen, Beverly, and Vickie.

Special thanks are due J. Patrick Wiseman, now of the Austin firm Richards, Wiseman, & Durst. Patrick was the main force in the *Howard S.* and *Hopkins* cases described herein. It has been my privilege to litigate with Patrick from 1978 to 1984 (when I joined Advocacy, Inc., Texas's protection and advocacy system for citizens with disabilities, for 4 years) and from 1988 to the present.

Special thanks are also due Mark S. Partin of Advocacy, Inc. Mark joined me in all my litigation from 1984 to 1988 and especially in those cases described in chapters 6 through 12. When we first began working together I tried to teach Mark all I knew and in the process learned from him more than I could ever have imagined.

Jones, Allen, and Fuquay in Dallas worked on the *Tatro* case from start to finish, with Craig Enoch beginning the case and leaving when appointed to the bench, and Charles Fuquay continuing until the very end. Jim Todd of Advocacy, Inc., shouldered the major burden in *Tatro* in the Second Circuit Court appeal and argued the case in the Supreme Court; Diane Shisk, also of Advocacy, Inc., had a major responsibility in the Supreme Court brief. Jesus Sifuentes orchestrated *Daniel R. R.* and let me join him at the district and circuit court levels. Donald Bayne, now of Van Nuys, California, and Henry Christopher of San Antonio did *Alamo Heights* and graciously accepted my amicus role at the circuit court. Advocacy, Inc.'s, Deborah Hiser, Renea Hicks, Jim Todd, and Diane Shisk had responsibility at various times for *Wilks* and *Griffith*.

Thanks are also due Dayle Bebee Aulds, now of El Campo, Texas, who created and ran Advocacy, Inc., from 1977 to 1988. Her early focus on children with disabilities established the climate for that agency to become a national leader in developing special education law. Thanks are certainly due Karen Steiner, my editor at Research Press, who made sure the manuscript made sense. A final thanks to Vivian Rice, my colleague and friend, who masquerades as a legal secretary and has bailed me out time after time since 1984.

# A Note About Citation Form

U.S.C. is *United States Code.*

C.F.R. is *Code of Federal Regulations.*

EHLR is the *Education for the Handicapped Law Report.*

F.Supp. is the *Federal Supplement,* in which federal district court opinions are published.

F.2d is the *Federal Reporter, 2nd Series,* in which federal circuit courts of appeals decisions are published.

U.S. is *U.S. Reports,* in which Supreme Court opinions are published.


Materials cited are available in most law libraries.

# Introduction

In the early 1970s, it was not unusual for schools to refuse to enroll children with disabilities or to place them in programs where they were totally segregated from nondisabled peers. Parents began going to court claiming that their children's Constitutional rights were being violated. A series of 37 decisions in federal courts confirmed that schools were unlawfully discriminating against these students, in violation of their rights under the Equal Protection and Due Process Clauses of the Fourteenth Amendment.

A series of Congressional hearings across the country convinced Congress that there was a nationwide problem and that a nationwide solution was needed. Congress took two approaches to solving this problem. The first approach recognized the civil rights of children with disabilities just as Congress had recognized the rights of those discriminated against because of race, color, creed, sex, or national origin.

In 1973 Congress amended the Rehabilitation Act by adding a section (commonly referred to as Section 504) that prohibited recipients of federal financial assistance from excluding disabled students from participating in, or being denied the benefits of, the school programs offered to others. Like other civil rights legislation, this new law contained no funds and, in fact, the penalty for noncompliance was the loss of other federal educational funds.

What would schools have to do to end discriminatory practices? The regulations that implement Section 504 made clear that schools must issue notice of rights, conduct appropriate evaluation, draft individual education plans, integrate students with disabilities into settings with nondisabled peers, and provide access to all extracurricular activities and student clubs. Further, a parent would have the right to complain about noncompliance to an independent hearing officer.

Section 504 has been amended several times since those regulations went into effect in 1977, but throughout this text I will simply refer to it the way courts do, as Section 504 of the Rehabilitation Act.

1

The second approach Congress took to this nationwide problem of school discrimination was a funding statute to help schools with the excess costs of special education. In 1975 Congress amended the Education of the Handicapped Act (EHA) with Public Law 94–142. That amendment was entitled the Education for All Handicapped Children Act. It was aimed at all the school-age children with disabilities, including approximately 1 million who were totally excluded from education and 2 million who were placed in inappropriate programs.

Congress provided that any state that wanted funds under this Act would have to abide by the new regulations and change its state laws to conform with those new regulations. All children would have to be served, regardless of the nature or severity of their handicapping condition. Parents would be given written notice of their rights and of actions proposed by the schools. Evaluation practices of schools would have to be reformed, and parents would have the right to seek an independent evaluation to contrast with the school's. Parents and school personnel would meet annually to put in writing the Individualized Education Program (IEP) plan that would govern services to the child. Schools would have to make available as needed related services such as physical therapy, occupational therapy, and school nursing services. Students with disabilities would be integrated with nondisabled students to the maximum extent appropriate. Finally, schools would have to agree to let an independent authority, an impartial hearing officer, rule on disputes and order needed changes in the school district's program.

As schools learned of these radical changes, everyone talked about Public Law 94–142 or the Education for All Handicapped Children Act. However, that was merely an amendment to the already existing EHA. Throughout this text I will refer to this funding law simply as the EHA. When I refer to just one of the Acts I will refer to it specifically. When I refer to "the Acts" or "these statutes" I will mean both the EHA (and all its amendments) and Section 504 (and all its amendments).

Both statutes have been the subject of much litigation from 1977 to date. Courts have added refinements, not spelled out in the statutes, in areas such as extending the school year into the summer months and extending the school day into the evening. The United States Supreme Court has ruled on these special education statutes, clarifying what appropriate education means and specifying the conditions under which parents can privately purchase services and force the school district to reimburse them.

Congress has amended these statutes several times, twice to overturn Supreme Court rulings that Congress felt conflicted with the statutes. In 1990 the EHA was amended further and its name changed to the Individuals with Disabilities Education Act (IDEA). The IDEA amendments are the most sweeping changes Congress has made since the passage of the Education for All Handicapped Children Act and will undoubtedly produce a wave of new litigation.

From 1977 to date, I have been fortunate to have had the chance to be involved in many of the court cases that have shaped and defined key issues associated with special education law. In my experience consulting with schools and parents, I have found that telling the stories behind these cases is the best way to explain the law. So, with the encouragement of my friends at Research Press—particularly Russell Pence and Ann Wendel—I have relived 10 cases in which I participated as counsel or amicus curiae (friend of the court).

The cases described in this book were selected to illustrate the basic principles one needs to understand special education law. Chapter 1 gives an overview of problems parents faced that caused Congress to act. Chapters 2 through 6 treat the need for evaluation, consider what is meant by appropriate education, show how the IEP plan must specially design the educational offering, examine the role of related services, and illustrate the requirement for services to be provided in the least restrictive environment. In chapters 7 and 8 we see how students qualify for extended school year and extended school day programs. Chapters 9 through 12 concern the responsibility of the state education agency, the importance of the impartial hearing officer, and the potential for parents to be reimbursed for educational costs and attorneys' fees.

Each of the cases selected obviously involved litigation: That is, the parents felt that the school was wrong enough that they had to sue. However, in these cases as in real life, the parents were not necessarily totally right and the school was not always totally wrong. As you will see in the following chapters, the parents did not win every time. What "won" were good procedure and good programming for children.

# Overview

I couldn't believe the story I was hearing from the couple seated on my office sofa. They had come to me simply because the private facility where their daughter was placed refused to let them see her records. But as I took them through a checklist of questions, we identified 22 categories of violations of federal law.

It became clear with this one child and her family why Congress had needed to pass the Education for All Handicapped Children Act in 1975. What we had begun would result in the first hearing in our state under that Act and the first education complaint in the nation under Section 504 of the Rehabilitation Act.

Jill was born with cerebral palsy, and as soon as it was properly diagnosed, her parents began to act. They exhausted themselves and their resources, crisscrossing their sprawling metropolitan area with daily trips to clinics and therapists and physicians. They soon developed a skepticism toward professionals. Many, though not all, of the professionals treated the parents with little respect, neither seeking their input nor listening to it. They gave directions for helping Jill, directions that were often impossible to follow within a 24-hour day. Worst of all, the professionals often disagreed, sending the parents in different and sometimes futile directions.

As I learned this family's story I could not believe they had never given up and said, "We're only parents; we can't be expected to do any more." Through them I learned what Congress had stumbled onto in developing the Education of the Handicapped Act (EHA): that parents are experts when it comes to their own child. They may not be able to make the diagnosis, but they are the only ones who can tell if the prescription is working or workable. Congress required parents to be involved in assessing the effectiveness of any program under the EHA. That is exactly what Jill's parents were trying to do when they asked to see their child's records.

When the EHA amendments went into effect in 1975, Jill was already eligible for special education services. She used a motorized wheelchair. She had limited use of her hands and arms. She had trouble sitting up straight in her chair. Her speech was soft and not very distinct. As she slumped in her wheelchair, head down, difficult to hear, many professionals assumed that she suffered retardation as one more effect of her cerebral palsy.

The school district in which Jill resided placed her, and all other children with orthopedic impairments, in private programs around town. The public school system paid some basic costs, but anything more, such as physical therapy, was up to the parents. There had been little evaluation of Jill, except what the parents had provided through their pediatrician. There were no stated goals for her. The parents had no idea what to expect. They had been counseled repeatedly to place their child in an institution so she would not be a burden on the family. The parents vigorously rejected that notion and any professional who suggested it, but what could they expect for Jill? How hard should they push her? How should they deal with her emotional growth or her resistance to trying new things? How far could she go? And where should they start?

One starting place that seemed obvious was physical therapy. Jill had little stamina and little strength. She could not use her hands to feed herself. Self-dressing was far beyond her reach. Transferring out of her wheelchair might never be something she could do by herself. But her parents could at least start, so they were paying for physical therapy at the center where Jill was placed.

When they saw no results, and when Jill seemed to indicate day after day that she had not seen the physical therapist, her parents asked to look at the records. They were getting regular billings, but they wanted to see whether Jill was getting regular therapy. The private facility refused, maintaining that the records were the therapist's private property.

On this first issue the remedy seemed simple. Jill had been placed at the private facility by her local public school, and school officials therefore had to ensure that this private placement was affording Jill all her federally established rights, including review of records. Otherwise the public school could not lawfully maintain that placement for Jill and would be obligated to find a different one. We let the public school and the private facility know our approach, but both simply told us that was not the way they chose to operate. (By the time our interactions had concluded, the public school had withdrawn all the children placed at that private facility, and the facility eventually closed.)

One question was whether Jill was receiving therapy. A second question was whether it was doing any good. In therapy sessions Jill was taken down a hall and placed on a floor mat, and a vibrator was run up and down her back. Without any agreed-upon goals, how could anyone tell if she was getting better or if she was getting enough therapy? What Jill needed was to be able to sit erect in her chair, to straighten her arms to reposition herself, to lift a book, to turn a page. How could anyone tell if the physical therapy was doing anything at all to meet those needs?

One other thing that Jill needed was to learn to grasp a pencil. She had not yet learned to write, and, at an age when other children would be at the third-grade level, she had been taught no mathematics. Her teacher at the center said that math could not be taught to a child who could not grasp a pencil. The teachers had written Jill off. It was time to write those teachers off and send Jill to a real school.

The logical place for Jill to be served was in her own public school, with children from her neighborhood. She had spent every day many miles from home in the private center. Given this fact and her mobility impairment, it was not surprising that she had not been able to make many friends. In addition to her very supportive parents Jill had an older brother and a younger sister, but she needed peer interaction. More important, she wanted friends—children from a neighborhood class who could drop by after school.

Approaching the school district about having Jill attend her home school was difficult. District officials felt that they had properly taken care of Jill, and the many other students like her, by putting her *somewhere*. They never considered keeping her inside their school system, let alone at a campus with nondisabled students. That segregationist attitude was literally etched in concrete: concrete curbs in front of the schools, concrete steps up to the buildings, concrete arrangement of inaccessible bathrooms.

The first step in asserting Jill's rights was to get an IEP planning meeting, run by the public school that was responsible for Jill's program. With the support of several other parents whose children were at the private center, we persuaded the school to schedule such a meeting. We asked for the written notice that would inform the parents of their rights and tell them what to expect at the meeting, but all we got was the date and time.

When we showed up for the IEP meeting, we were surprised to see all the other parents there, too. It was a group IEP session. One school official was there with mimeographed IEP forms—only the children's names were different. The forms had been prepared on the basis of what the public school had already contracted with the private center to provide: available classes, available therapies, a school day of a predetermined length, and so forth. Nothing was based on the individual needs of a child. The 12 sets of parents in the room were given 20 minutes to ask questions about how the program would be carried out, but nothing in the IEP could be changed.

When I tried to enter the room with Jill's parents, the public school official blocked my way. She said that the meeting was only for parents and teachers. No teachers were there, and I asked her what category she belonged in. She simply closed the door. I went to a pay phone and called the Director of the Division of Assistance to States at the federal Bureau of Education for the Handicapped and stated my complaint. I later learned that when the public school official returned to her downtown office she found a telephone inquiry from Washington on her desk. To my knowledge, that school district has never held another group IEP meeting or barred another person accompanying a parent.

But we were still not getting anywhere. Jill's IEP was based on continued placement at the private center. No evaluation was to be performed. Why bother? The school officials already knew in advance what was available and what would be offered, so why conduct an evaluation? Moreover, evaluation might expose a need they did not plan to meet.

The parents obtained an independent evaluation. On the basis of Jill's needs and her potential for growth, that evaluation recommended daily physical and occupational therapy, given in individual 30-minute sessions by a licensed therapist. The private center offered only as much therapy as the parents were willing to pay for. Even if we were to get Jill served by the public school, school officials had let us know they would not give her what our evaluation indicated. Their physical and occupational therapy services were contracted out through a county consulting agreement. Physical therapy was offered twice a week: either on Monday and Thursday or on Tuesday and Friday; Wednesday was reserved for paperwork. We were told that no one would receive therapy more than 2 days per week and 5 days per week was an impossibility.

But the real mystery was Jill's intellectual potential. She had been treated by the school and the center as if she had severe mental limitations. She was often left unattended to slump in her chair, often not looking others in the eye, unable to speak loudly. Regular tests would not work for Jill (although that did not deter the school from trying them). She moved her hands too slowly to point to objects within allotted time segments, and she could not read or write quickly. When we arranged appropriate testing, it revealed more than we had expected: Jill's intelligence was in the superior range.

With this information, the school was more responsive during the next try at an IEP meeting. Jill was to attend a regular elementary school in her public school district. The school building would be made accessible. But Jill's teacher was not at the IEP meeting. No one from the school transportation department attended the meeting to explain how the all-important special transportation would work for this young lady in a heavy motorized wheelchair. The parents were told if they had any problems, they would have to contact the transportation department directly because the special education officials had no authority over transportation. And the IEP form developed by the public school left too many unanswered questions about class scheduling, therapy times, and physical education.

Jill's parents were asked repeatedly what they wanted to drop from the curriculum to make time for the therapy sessions. When we replied that Jill was entitled to education *and* related services, not education *or* related services, we could tell by the reaction that scheduling was up in the air.

As the school year started, one of the things Jill seemed excited about was entering a school cafeteria and going through a lunch line (which at this point was inaccessible to a wheelchair user). She had heard her brother and sister talk about school lunchtime, and I realized again how abnormal her education had been up to now. No typical peers, no normal expectations, no school to identify with, no extracurricular activities, not even a school cafeteria. And I realized again how remarkable Jill and her parents were. With all the misinformation given them by professionals and all the mistreatment by school personnel, nothing had lessened their optimism and their willingness to keep trying.

During this process, we had filed a complaint with the federal Office for Civil Rights (OCR) under Section 504 of the Rehabilitation Act. I received a phone call from Washington explaining that this was the first such complaint received and that everyone would proceed through the situation with a great deal of caution and scrutiny. We were raising issues for the first time: Did Section 504 require an evaluation, as the EHA did? Was the IEP requirement the same? Were related services required under Section 504 the same as those specified in the EHA? The answer for Jill could become the answer for the country.

One issue, that the bus ride to school was so long as to be debilitating and countereducational, was the type that Section 504 could really address. What kind of bus rides did the nondisabled students face? How long were they? Were the students with disabilities getting unequal treatment? Did their buses regularly arrive after classes had started and leave before the full school day was completed? The OCR investigator asked the school district to produce the bus routes for all students in the district, those with and without disabilities, so that average routes could be constructed and comparisons made. Rather than produce such costly paperwork, the school district agreed to change Jill's route.

The EHA also offered a possible remedy for some of these problems—a step that Congress called an impartial due process hearing—and we requested one. No such hearings had yet been held in our state, and the state education agency had not even given local schools guidance on how to conduct them. Jill's school district selected a former consultant as a hearing officer, and we began to prepare our case. We wanted an order to go back to the IEP table with a new IEP form and with all necessary and appropriate personnel present at the meeting. We wanted to leave that meeting with everything completed.

We also wanted a full evaluation of Jill's occupational therapy and physical therapy needs. Because the public school did not want to have to provide that therapy, it had, logically, refused to evaluate for those needs. This placed the school's evaluator in the rather difficult position of explaining to a hearing officer how, under both the EHA and Section 504, the school had performed a comprehensive evaluation of a student who used a wheelchair and could not grasp a pencil and somehow had missed the fact that she needed physical therapy.

The school district was represented in the hearing by an attorney widely recognized as a national expert on school law. His associate has since gained her own national reputation as an attorney, hearing officer, congressional witness, and counsel to national school organizations. I have often explained to clients that the better the attorney representing the school, the better the result we would obtain. No client ever believes this, but it is true. In this case, we were doubly blessed.

Our preparation and the records we shared with the other side led to such ready agreement that the hearing was just a dress rehearsal for our consensus. I was so anxious to complete the hearing that my questioning of witnesses was not in good form. At one break I asked the senior attorney for the school district if he felt that I was leading my witnesses too much, and he wryly commented, "Herding them is more like it." But we did conclude quickly.

The hearing was not between adversaries. We could sense the interest with which some school personnel faced the challenge of the first wheelchair user in the district and the excitement of exploring Jill's intellectual potential. But we did lose a few friends with our insistence on a new IEP form. School district officials had printed a 2-year supply, and forcing them to revise it was a real bureaucratic blow.

The highlight of the hearing for me was the good-humored testimony of the teacher who had by now been seeing Jill daily for a few weeks. I asked her if she had received any training about the

IEP process, and she replied no. I asked if she had been invited to Jill's IEP meeting, and she said no. I asked if she would have attended had she been invited, and she said no. I asked if she had been sent a copy of the IEP plan after the meeting, and she said no. I asked if she would have done anything different in the classroom if she had received a copy, and she said, "No, I would have filed it with all the other trash I get from Central Office."

We got our order to return to a new IEP meeting. At one point during that meeting, the school district proposed an annual goal for Jill that seemed very high. To support the notion of Jill's potential in that area, the teacher pulled out an example of Jill's writing, done after only a few weeks of exposure to real education. I know I saw a tear in Jill's mother's eye. The opportunity for which Jill's parents had worked so hard for 8 years was finally beginning.

Jill's case shows how correct Congress was in detailing the specific protections of the EHA. We need parental involvement if the process is to work. Parents need to be able to work through one central local school district for evaluations, records, and services rather than being sent around to different agencies. Parents need written notice in advance of meetings so they will know what is to be considered and when, and so they can be informed partners in the decision-making process.

Students must have full evaluations, including medical diagnostics, or programming can never be appropriate. Each evaluation must be free of prejudice about what is available and what the school would like to offer the student, as opposed to what that one child actually needs. Parents need the safeguard of an independent evaluation when they distrust the appropriateness of the school district's evaluation.

The IEP must have clear, evaluation-based baselines as starting points, as well as annual goals with short-term measures that let parents tell if the program is producing results. All decisions must be responsive to the unique needs of the child in question—not based on what the school has chosen to make available in the district. Instruction, therapy, and other related services need to be governed by the written IEP plan.

Congress gave the IEP committee the authority to allocate those resources: making a building accessible, assigning a physical therapist, changing a bus route, and so forth. The services offered must not be limited by the parents' ability to pay but must meet the child's needs at no cost to the parents. Inaccessibility should never be allowed to bar a student from a school building, or a lunch line, or a science lab.

Parents must be involved in assessing the effectiveness of their child's program. To that end, they must have full access to all records collected, maintained, or used by the school district in regard to their child. Finally, when parents' complaints cannot be resolved with the school, an impartial hearing officer must be able to order any change that is justified. All of those rights are specified by the federal special education laws, and Jill's case certainly shows why each one is important.

After President Reagan's election, he and Vice President Bush targeted the EHA and Section 504 for major revisions. Their proposals would have largely abolished the role that parents like Jill's had played in challenging school districts. The federal Department of Education held official hearings on the Reagan-Bush proposals around the country. The first such hearing provoked a near riot when it was held in an inaccessible building and many witnesses could not attend. The official hearing site for our state was surrounded by mounted police who said that they had been told to expect trouble.

Jill's parents, and others in a group they had formed called the Association for Rights of Children with Handicaps, held a people's hearing in the state's largest city to voice their opposition. Nearly 200 parents attended. Jill was our lead speaker, and she had prepared a beautiful statement. But I had underestimated the impact of the television station's cameras and lights and the size of the crowd, and I was unable to coax anything from my reluctant witness. Jill's mother stepped in and asked if there was anything Jill would like to tell the federal government and these people. Jill replied in loud and clear tones, "Don't ever let them put me back in that other place."

The efforts of Jill's parents and others across the country prompted written comments to the White House—reportedly the largest number of comments ever received by the federal government about a proposed change in regulations. The White House later admitted that the comments were 95 percent negative. The proposed changes were dropped, and Congress amended the EHA to prevent future regulatory change without legislative approval.

Although Jill's war had been won, the battles continued. Transportation was never easy. As she progressed from elementary to middle school and then to high school, the change of buildings brought threats of moving Jill away from her neighborhood schools to centralized facilities for students with disabilities.

Continuation of Jill's physical and occupational therapy was resisted every year as therapists claimed that she had reached her potential and that services should thus be stopped. Attempts were made to push the burden of physical therapy onto the parents in a home program that was beyond the competence of unlicensed personnel: The range-of-motion exercises proposed could have caused permanent damage if done incorrectly. When Jill fell short of her goals, her parents were blamed at the IEP meeting for not doing their part.

Jill was told to stay home from school on a day when standardized tests were to be administered throughout the district. District officials obviously wanted "the handicapped" excluded from the testing process so scores would be higher—missing the point that Jill's performance might have raised the average. Jill's mother fixed that problem districtwide, and the state was eventually forced to adopt a statewide rule. Complaints about the accessibility of the science labs brought an offer to waive Jill's science requirements, but this college-bound student did not want a waiver: She wanted science.

Thanks to the perseverance of Jill and her parents, their efforts paid off. Jill is now in college, completing a degree in psychology.

# Evaluation

Evaluation must be the basis for all educational programming. Without it, the school cannot know how to accommodate the child and the teacher cannot know what to do differently in the classroom. Without evaluation, the parents cannot learn what their child's needs are. (Congress was very clear, as the legislative history shows, that evaluation is meant in part to teach parents how they can better understand and help their children and can assist their schools by complementing in-school activities.) Finally, without good evaluation there can be no goal setting for the child and no real assessment of whether the child is benefiting adequately from the programming.

To place a child in an ongoing program without evaluation—and simply to have the teacher do for that child what is done for all the other children—might result in the child's getting nothing. The child might consequently become so frustrated that he or she would begin to exhibit problem behaviors. Then the school, instead of focusing on solving the child's educational problem, would concentrate on disciplinary sanctions, and the child would start down a one-way street toward total educational failure. That seemed to be what was happening to Douglas. The remedy was evaluation.

I had thought that the evaluation requirements of the Education of the Handicapped Act (EHA) and of Section 504 of the Rehabilitation Act were fairly straightforward. The child had to be evaluated before school personnel could begin programming.[1] The parents were to be involved in that evaluation process.[2] The child had to be evaluated in all areas related to the suspected disability,[3] with such evaluation including medical diagnostic services if needed.[4] The evaluation team was to include at least one specialist with knowledge in the area of the suspected disability.[5]

Once conducted, the evaluation was to be kept current to make sure the program was responsive to changing needs. Reevaluation was required at least every 3 years,[6] but it also had to occur when a parent[7]

15

or a teacher requested it[8] or when conditions warranted.[9] Further, before the school proposed a significant change in placement, such as a severe disciplinary sanction, a reevaluation had to occur.[10] Whenever a parent disagreed with the school's evaluation, the parent could procure an independent evaluation, which the school had to consider in programming decisions.[11]

Finally, the evaluation process would be ongoing, assessing the effectiveness of the agreed-upon IEP plan. Parents were to be involved in that assessment as well. When parents thought that more evaluation was needed for an effective program, they could request it of the school. If the school refused, the parents were entitled to a written justification for the refusal.[12]

Unfortunately, schools in our state had been misled about these new responsibilities. The state education agency opposed the federal laws. The state school board called on our state's congressional delegation to repeal the 1975 amendments to the EHA, the Education for All Handicapped Children Act. The state education agency held workshops around the state (I attended three) telling local school districts that the federal laws were copied from the laws of our state and that a local district could be in compliance with the new federal laws simply by complying with existing state laws. That was not true.

The importance of those new responsibilities regarding evaluation is illustrated in Douglas's case.[13] Douglas had contracted meningitis when he was a year old, and his first school suspected that a mild neurological disability had resulted. Douglas was classified as having minimal brain dysfunction, a catch-all designation popular at the time. (Years later he still carried that label and was served in regular classes with a resource teacher.)

Douglas had increasing difficulty in school. What exactly was the problem? Had there really been a childhood neurological trauma? Were there residual effects that hindered learning? Did Douglas have an auditory processing problem, a visual processing problem, or both? Perhaps he could process information correctly but could not store it properly. Or if he could store it properly, maybe he could not recall it correctly. Or perhaps he could recall it correctly if asked to do so orally but not if asked to write it down—or vice versa. Or perhaps he could respond perfectly if he just had some extra time. Had Douglas suffered an impact on the area of the brain that controlled impulses? Was that related to his increasing misbehaviors? Would normal disciplinary sanctions produce appropriate responses or be counterproductive?

Douglas's evaluation had labeled him, but it had not helped school personnel in any way to program differently for him. His teacher did not know how to help. In one document filed with the court a school official said that it was virtually impossible to keep Douglas in class, that the school had exhausted all alternatives in trying to reach him, and that he definitely needed special help.

The first step in offering that special help would be an evaluation that would help both the teacher and the parents understand how to reach Douglas. In a document read during the trial, one teacher reported feeling that Douglas was in the middle of a lake, trying to swim for shore, but did not know which direction to take. She added that she felt as if she were in there with him.

The parents asked for evaluation, but the school officials refused. They said that state law only required evaluation every 3 years and that it would be quite a few months before Douglas would be re-evaluated. His problems seemed mild, but they were slowly getting worse. He was beginning to misbehave in the classroom and was accumulating 1- and 2-day in-school suspensions. Not surprisingly, his attendance became erratic.

An earlier court decision in Pennsylvania dealing with students having learning disabilities seemed to describe Douglas's problem:

> A learning disabled child may look normal and use language in a way that is typical for his age, yet any of the methods used in the regular classroom to teach him how to read may get nowhere. . . . As they grow older, children with learning disabilities who are not helped are likely to continue falling behind in their school work. . . . A hard-working student can regress. Failure can cause frustration, loss of self-esteem, and antagonism towards adults.[14]

In many such situations, a remarkable teacher can reach a child through instinct and by drawing on past experiences. But that connection lasts only as long as the student has that particular teacher. When Douglas left such a teacher and moved to high school, conditions worsened quickly. As the court noted, any success "ended abruptly," and "he immediately began to develop behavior problems, characterized by truancy and wandering in the halls."[15] These problems were seen as disciplinary infractions, to be dealt with by so-called regular education. No school officials discussed these problems with special education teachers or considered them conditions that would warrant further evaluation.[16]

The EHA also required the school to maintain a comprehensive system of personnel development that would enable school personnel, when faced with a child whom no one seemed to know how to reach, to "acquire and disseminate . . . promising educational practices."[17] Court records noted that Douglas exhibited a short attention span, hyperactivity, and demands for attention. What had that one successful teacher done to reach Douglas? What must the high school teachers learn to do to make their program work? Apparently no one asked, or answered, those questions. Douglas spent increasing amounts of time in disciplinary settings when he was in school and increasing numbers of days absent from school.

His parents turned to an independent source for help with evaluation. Shortly thereafter an incident occurred at school, upsetting Douglas so much that he left immediately. When his parents found him at home he seemed so agitated that they contacted their outside diagnostician, who recommended that Douglas be served in a residential setting.[18] The parents, knowing that the public school program was not working, followed their independent expert's advice and placed Douglas in a private school. The costs of that schooling exceeded the parents' insurance coverage, and they sought an attorney's help to keep Douglas in an appropriate setting at public expense.

Douglas's parents tried to reason with the public school officials one more time. They asked for an IEP meeting to discuss their son's needs. The school held such a meeting, without notifying the parents, and dropped Douglas from its rolls for excessive absences. When the parents informed the school that Douglas was not truant from school but was rather being served in a private school, the public school dismissed him because he had "moved."[19]

We argued that Douglas's needs were fairly simple but that neglect had allowed his situation to worsen. What was needed was evaluation, followed by a program based on the results of that evaluation. Even a child with mild problems, if not properly evaluated, will be the subject of poor programming. We asked for evaluation and were refused. We asked for a new IEP meeting and were refused. We asked for an impartial hearing and were given one—with the school district's attorney chairing the meeting and the superintendent as hearing officer![20]

We complained to the state education agency, which replied that it had no responsibilities in this case. The state had not set up a system to provide for impartial due process hearings as was required by law.[21] We wanted the state to do so. The state also was required to investigate complaints,[22] but it refused to do so.[23]

We complained to the federal office for special education programs. The ensuing argument over the state's failure to implement the required hearing system led to the withholding of federal special education funds from the state. Finally, we complained to the federal Office for Civil Rights, whose investigation was unfortunately so slow that it produced an opinion days after the court had ruled in this case. With all these complaints, the court found that we had taken all reasonable and practicable steps to exhaust our administrative remedies.[24]

We felt that our only remaining option was to file suit in federal court. We were running out of time. Douglas's private school had warned that it might have to discharge him for failure to pay his bills. We met with the judge, who would not grant a temporary restraining order but who set the matter for full trial on whether to grant an injunction. The trial was set for only a few days hence. This indicated that the judge took us very seriously because at the time, that federal district had the fourth busiest civil litigation docket in the United States. The judge said that he had not heard of any of the federal special education laws we were talking about, but he was willing to give us priority.

When we arrived in court, I realized the enormity of what we had begun. These federal Acts were very new. There had been only two or three decisions under this legislation, and those had been on fairly narrow procedural issues. We were raising a full range of issues. Some of the facts in our case had occurred before the Education for All Handicapped Children Act had gone into effect on October 1, 1977, so we were relying heavily on Section 504 of the Rehabilitation Act and on the EHA, which had been in force since 1974.[25]

In our lawsuit we claimed that the school had failed to give appropriate notice under the Acts. We claimed that more comprehensive evaluation was required, with different personnel and at different times than what the school district had done. We claimed that the IEP was defective. We claimed that inappropriate programming had forced a private residential placement rather than allowing Douglas to be served in the least restrictive environment. We claimed that he had been illegally disciplined because the school had not related his misbehaviors to his inappropriate placement. We claimed that, even though the parents had unilaterally made the residential placement, the school should be forced to reimburse them for past expenses and continue the placement at public expense. We claimed that services to Douglas should continue during the summer months. We claimed that our right to an impartial hearing had been violated and that the state education agency had violated our rights by not investigating our complaint. Finally, we wanted to recover our attorneys' fees.

We had raised practically every issue, and it suddenly struck me that we could lose on every one. We had asked for the first comprehensive examination of these Acts by a federal judge, an examination that could result in a weakening of the rights of 4 million school children with disabilities just as these laws were beginning to be implemented.

When I walked into court, the representative of the attorney general's office approached me and asked if we could talk. He said that he knew I was interested in test litigation but wondered if I would be willing to settle. I said, "Of course." He said, "What would it take for you to settle?" I said, "Compliance with the law." He said, "I knew you were just interested in test litigation" and went back to his seat.

An official from the office of the state director of special education then came up to me. He dramatically pulled his airline ticket from his pocket and showed me the time of his return flight. He said, "Your case is going to be laughed out of court, and I'll be back in my office in time to go to lunch so all of us can laugh at you." I meant to check with him during the fourth full day of trial to see how he was enjoying it.

The introductory statements from the local school district and the attorney general's office were very confusing in regard to the applicable law. They cited the wrong public laws, referred to the wrong statutory citations, and cited the wrong regulations. I mentioned that to my co-counsel, and he told me to correct the other attorneys each time to make sure the court was not misled. We knew from our meeting on the temporary restraining order that this judge had not previously heard these statutes argued. There were no other federal district court decisions to use as guidance on the wide range of issues we were raising, so we at least wanted the court to have everything referred to correctly.

After I had interrupted the other attorneys several times, the judge asked, "Are you an expert in this area?" My co-counsel knew exactly what to do. At the next opportunity he called me to the witness stand and began asking the questions needed to qualify me as an expert. He then asked me to explain the law. I was already anxious enough that we were raising so many issues for the first time in any federal court and could lose. But now I had to realize that a loss could result from my own testimony in the trial. I had always taken great pains to prepare witnesses before trial, and now I was trying to remember my own advice. I have served as an expert witness in trials since then, but being my own witness seemed odd.

The best thing about being a witness in this position was that I was cross-examined by the attorneys for the other side. Their questions gave me an opportunity to debate the issues and to argue what the law was and how it should be applied. That is something usually reserved for briefing after the trial, and it was wonderful to have that opportunity mid-trial.

I felt we were making our case that the schools were not doing what should reasonably be expected under the relatively new legislation, but the judge had already decided how he would like to see that question addressed. He told the attorneys to approach the bench, and all six of us stood in front of him. The courtroom was nearly filled with spectators, including school officials from neighboring districts who saw the obvious implications of this case for their own districts. One of the spectators was the special education director in the city where the trial was being held. She was a friend of the judge, and, fortunately, I knew her as well because she had used me as a consultant in her district.

The judge began by saying to us in hushed tones, "I don't want to tell you how to run your case, but . . . ," and I knew he was going to tell us exactly what he wanted us to do. He said that his friend the special education director was in the audience and that he would like to know what her district was doing under these laws. He asked if anyone knew her. When I replied that I did, he asked if I would consider calling her as an expert witness. All six attorneys pivoted at the same time and looked at that elegant lady, and she slid nearly out of sight. The court called a brief recess, and I asked her to appear. She telephoned her superintendent, who must have wondered what was going on, and then took the stand.

She could have ended the case at that point. She could have said that it was not really fair to expect a school to comply with these new laws. She could have said that the defendant school district was doing about as well as anyone else. She could have said that her own school district was not doing any better. But she didn't. She very patiently explained exactly how her district would have dealt with a youngster like Douglas, and I think we won our trial at that point.

On Friday afternoon the judge called the bailiff and sent him out with a note. We all seemed curious, so the judge explained that he was making sure the air-conditioning would stay on because he knew that we would go well past 5 P.M. on Friday and continue on Saturday. This judge was going to give us all the time we needed to see if we could make our case.

One of the points in the testimony that seemed to strike the judge as singularly important was when we asked a witness what Douglas's prognosis would be in the absence of appropriate programming. The answer was that, with his worsening behavioral pattern, he would probably end up incarcerated. On the other hand, with an appropriate program, Douglas would have quite a good prognosis because his handicaps were educationally related and were relatively mild.[26] When the trial concluded, I felt certain that the judge was going to order whatever programming was necessary to give Douglas that chance.

Only a few days later, the judge called all the attorneys back into court to read his decision, a rather unusual step that underscored how seriously he took this case and its implications for the development of these new laws. I was in Boston conducting a special education conference, so my co-counsel read the decision to me over the phone. I could not believe it. We had won every single thing we had asked for.

The court ordered "an immediate and comprehensive evaluation of Douglas to determine his special educational needs."[27] The evaluation was to be "conducted by a competent, independent, professional evaluator."[28] After that evaluation, the local school was to "immediately develop an individual educational plan which specifies Douglas' needs and all the services required to meet those needs."[29] The local school district was then to provide appropriate educational services for Douglas in the least restrictive environment.[30]

Douglas was to remain in the private school, at public expense, until the local school could provide a program. The local school was also to reimburse the parents for expenses incurred at the private school up to that date.[31] The state education agency defendants were ordered to comply with the procedural safeguards outlined in the federal law and, specifically, to create an impartial due process hearing officer system.[32]

The local school district moved immediately to comply. It hired new counsel to evaluate the case and determine whether it should be appealed. The new counsel decided to settle the case and worked quickly to bring the client into compliance. The result was that Douglas came home to an appropriate program, and the family received counseling at school district expense to help him reintegrate into the family setting.

Douglas graduated with his regular education class. Programming based on appropriate evaluation was all that was really needed.

## Notes

1. 34 C.F.R. 300.531.
2. See, for example, 34 C.F.R. 300.504(a), 504(b)(1), 505(a)(3), and 534(b).
3. 34 C.F.R. 300.532(f).
4. 34 C.F.R. 300.13(a).
5. 34 C.F.R. 300.532(e).
6. 34 C.F.R. 300.534(b).
7. 34 C.F.R. 300.534(b).
8. 34 C.F.R. 300.534(b).
9. 34 C.F.R. 300.534(b).
10. 34 C.F.R. 104.35(a).
11. 34 C.F.R. 300.503.
12. 34 C.F.R. 300.504(a)(2), 505(a)(2)–(4).
13. Howard S. v. Friendswood Independent School District and Texas Education Agency, 454 F. Supp. 634 (S.D. TX 1978).
14. Frederick L. v. Thomas, 419 F.Supp. 960 (E.D. PA 1976), at 963.
15. Howard S., at 635.

16. Howard S., at 635–636.
17. 34 C.F.R. 300.380.
18. Howard S., at 635.
19. Howard S., at 636.
20. Howard S., at 637.
21. 34 C.F.R. 300.508.
22. 34 C.F.R. 300.602, now found at 34 C.F.R. 76.780–783.
23. Howard S., at 638.
24. Howard S., at 638.
25. Howard S., at 637.
26. Howard S., at 635–636.
27. Howard S., at 642.
28. Howard S., at 642.
29. Howard S., at 642.
30. Howard S., at 642.
31. Howard S., at 642.
32. Howard S., at 643.

# Appropriate Education

It took several years for cases under the Education of the Handicapped Act (EHA) and Section 504 of the Rehabilitation Act to reach courts and produce judicial opinions. Schools, parents, and attorneys were watching each new opinion to see where the lines might be drawn. The EHA certainly provided a floor of opportunity, but how high was the ceiling? Was the EHA just a false promise that would unduly raise parents' expectations, as President Ford had said when he reluctantly signed it into law? Or was it so all-encompassing that no school could really afford to implement it fully?

The key word in the EHA was *appropriate*. Every eligible child with a disability was to be afforded a free, appropriate public education. But how much was required for a program to be appropriate? One case began to work its way through the courts on that most basic issue.

That case, *Board of Education v. Rowley*,[1] involved a first-grader named Amy who had a profound hearing impairment. She was the only hearing-impaired child in her school. Her parents both had hearing impairments and used sign language. She had begun to respond to sign language at an early age, although she also seemed to interact well with hearing and speaking peers.

When Amy went to kindergarten, the school put her in a regular classroom to determine how she would perform. The parents felt strongly that Amy would need a sign language interpreter in order to do well in school. At the parents' request a sign language interpreter was employed for 2 weeks. He reported to the school at the end of that period that, in his opinion, Amy did not need his services.

When Amy started first grade, school officials used all available information to formulate her IEP plan. Amy could read lips, so her position in the classroom was important. She could process some verbal information through the use of hearing aids. However, she needed training in synthesizing the information she got from a variety of sources: lipreading, sign language, and hearing aids. She would not understand all of the information, so she needed some extra help. Finally, her expressive speech was weak, so she needed special assistance in that area.

The school developed a full IEP plan that called for (a) inclusion in a regular class, (b) 1 hour daily instruction from a tutor who was a certified teacher of the deaf, (c) 3 hours weekly speech therapy, and (d) use of a wireless microphone in the classroom (tuned to Amy's FM hearing aids) so that Amy could hear the teacher and her classmates even when she could not read their lips. In addition, the school officials installed a teletype machine so that they could interact more easily with Amy's parents, and three officials took sign language courses.

At the IEP meeting, the school also considered Amy's social needs. In instances where a child functions adequately academically but shows problems in social interaction, some schools will argue that social skills are not their responsibility or concern. In this case, however, school officials correctly considered social interaction an integral part of education and found that Amy was achieving educationally, academically, and socially. Consequently, they did not feel that Amy needed a sign language interpreter for any aspect of her school day.

Amy's parents strongly disagreed and took the issue of a sign language interpreter to an impartial hearing. The hearing officer upheld the school district's position. However, on appeal, the federal district court and circuit court of appeals agreed with the parents. Those courts found that Amy, with an IQ of 122, should have been doing better than merely achieving passing grades. They found that her "energy and eagerness" were not spent in achievement but rather were used to compensate for her disability.[2]

In the federal district court,[3] it was revealed that Amy could not process approximately 40 percent of the words spoken in the classroom. The court saw that as an access issue. If Amy were physically barred from the classroom 40 percent of the day because of a disability, everyone would agree that was discrimination. Similarly, if she were forced to turn off her hearing aids for 40 percent of each day, this would illegally deny her access to education. Thus, it appeared to the court that it was discriminatory not to do whatever was needed to allow Amy access to 100 percent of what was being said in the classroom.

The school argued, to the contrary, that although Amy might miss a portion of what was being said at a given moment, the instructional program in its totality—classroom instruction, FM hearing aids, daily tutoring, and speech therapy—gave Amy enough to provide an equal opportunity.

Prior to Amy's case, the most complete definition of appropriate education had come in *Armstrong v. Kline*.[4] The *Armstrong* court had found that an appropriate education was one that would allow a child, within the limits of the disability, to become self-sufficient and stay out of the care of an institution. How could that standard be applied across the board? Amy was clearly headed for self-sufficiency; she was not going to end up in an institution. Did that mean that the school was not obligated to do anything for her?

The lower courts dealing with Amy's case found that a lot more had to be done.[5] They said that the EHA required the school to maximize the child's potential. With her 122 IQ, Amy had a lot of potential. How much more would the school have to do to maximize it?

School districts across the country were upset by the implications of that standard. Many felt that the duty to maximize potential would drain all the resources of the public schools. Schools envisioned enormously expensive programs geared to producing maximum results for a single child with a severe disability. The standard adopted in Amy's case—opportunity to achieve full potential commensurate with the opportunity provided to other children—seemed to be a blank check.

To parents and advocacy organizations, the standard developed in the circuit court of appeals in Amy's case seemed fair. Why not give their children the same chance as other children? The fact that it cost more to equalize opportunity for these children should not cause them to lose all of their rights.

At that point the United States Supreme Court agreed that there was confusion among the circuit courts and agreed to hear Amy's case. All of us involved in special education law held our breaths. The Supreme Court had not yet interpreted the EHA. In its first consideration of that law, the Supreme Court might find it to be an unconstitutional federal intrusion into state and local educational affairs. Much of the debate over appropriateness hinged on interpretation of the regulations promulgated to implement the EHA. The Supreme Court could announce that those regulations were too far-reaching and not reasonably related to the purposes of the Act and strike them down. Or the Supreme Court could decide that cost was a factor to consider in deciding how much programming was appropriate, giving schools with scarce resources an argument that they need not do more because they cannot afford to do more.

Several of us attorneys active in special education law called a meeting in Washington, D.C., to plan amicus curiae briefs to inform the Supreme Court of the implications of the arguments it would soon hear. Two central policy questions would be raised. First, appropriate education must be sufficient to make a difference in the life of a child with a disability, but this relatively new federal statute could not bankrupt school districts without causing swift congressional backlash and amendment. Proponents of the maximization standard were cautioned that they might win the battle in the Supreme Court and lose the war in Congress.

The second issue was equally tough. How could one fashion a single standard for appropriateness that would serve the incredibly diverse population of 4½ million students with disabilities? How could a student with severe mental impairment and other multiple disabilities residing at a state school be on the same standard as a college-bound high school student with a learning disability? Would a single standard be so watered down that it would not really help either end of the spectrum? There was no unanimity, as each advocate wanted the adoption of a standard that would favor his or her particular group.

The argument before the Supreme Court was as dramatic as the issues. Amy's attorney also had a hearing impairment. There are few things more lively, adrenalin pumping, and totally draining than the rapid give-and-take between the attorneys arguing a case and the nine justices hearing it. But how does one enter into that exchange if one is hearing impaired?

The Supreme Court, for the first time in its history, created a technological aid for an attorney. A computer monitor was placed on the lectern. A stenographer keyed in every word from the justices, and their words appeared instantly on the screen. When Amy's attorney spoke, he looked at the justices. As soon as a justice interrupted with a question, the attorney looked down at the screen to read the question. What more beautiful way to symbolize Amy's needs and potential than to have such a representative hold his own at this summit of verbal warfare.

After a few months of waiting, we got the decision.[6] What Justice Rehnquist wrote for the majority in the Supreme Court opinion in *Rowley* squared with the last decade of court cases interpreting the term *appropriate*.

Congress, in developing the EHA, had relied heavily on the seminal case of *Pennsylvania Association for Retarded Children v. Commonwealth of Pennsylvania*.[7] That case held that students with retardation could no longer be excluded from public instruction. The offering that was required for each child was one that was appropriate to his or her learning capacities. And thus we had a standard: appropriateness.

Following soon thereafter, two other cases decided by that same federal district court in Pennsylvania added important clarifications. *Fialkowski v. Shapp*[8] concerned two 6-year-olds who had severe retardation but were offered age-appropriate first-grade prereading activities. When the parents complained, the attorney for the school district stated that those children were being given everything that the nondisabled students were offered and that their duty was merely to provide classroom space. The school district argued that the term *appropriate* was surplusage not susceptible to interpretation.

The Fialkowskis' attorney responded that the children had been given access to buildings, rooms, and playschool but they had been denied access to education. The plaintiffs' argument was that they were denied equal protection under the Constitution because, unlike the programs offered to nondisabled children, the nature of the educational programs offered them was such that no chance existed that the programs would confer benefit.

In its finding for the plaintiffs, *Fialkowski* established that the student with a disability must stand a realistic chance of benefiting from the offering if it is to be called appropriate.

The second case decided by that federal district court, *Frederick L. v. Thomas*,[9] dealt with learning disabled children facing this same problem. The court summarized their contention:

> Most of the plaintiffs are afforded access to the same curriculum as normal children, but it is argued that the test of equal treatment is the suitability of the instructional services for the educational needs of the child. Many of the plaintiffs, it is said, cannot derive any educational benefit from the normal curriculum if that experience is not mediated by special instruction aimed at their learning handicaps.

In finding for the plaintiffs, the court established in *Frederick L.* that the instructional program must be tailored to the specific child's needs sufficiently to provide educational benefit before the offering can be called appropriate.

This requirement—to tailor the special education offering to the child in order to make the education appropriate—was adopted in Amy's case by the Supreme Court, which noted Congress's concern that many students with disabilities "were left to fend for themselves in classrooms designed for education of their nonhandicapped peers."[10] Refusing to individually design the offering in those classrooms is unacceptable: "Furnishing handicapped children with only such services as are available to nonhandicapped children would in all probability fall short of the statutory requirement of free appropriate public education."[11]

Not only must the services be different from those offered the nondisabled, but for each child with a disability the offering must be individualized or personalized: "The free appropriate public education required by the Act is tailored to the unique needs of the handicapped child."[12]

What of the access argument—that Amy was being barred from the classroom by her disability? The Supreme Court found that access to education was required for students with disabilities. But must the school do any more than just open the door and grant bare access? The answer is yes. The Court specified that an appropriate educational offering be one sufficient "to make such access meaningful" and that "the education to which access is provided be sufficient to confer some educational benefit upon the handicapped child."[13]

For the Supreme Court in *Rowley* the essential question became "Is the individualized educational program developed through the Act's procedures reasonably calculated to enable the child to receive educational benefits?"[14]

What is "reasonably calculated"? According to Amy's parents, anything short of a sign language interpreter was unreasonable. They assumed that the program would not work. But the prevailing standard seems to have been enunciated by Justice Blackmun in his concurring opinion: "The question is whether Amy's program, viewed as a whole, offered her an opportunity to understand and participate in the classroom that was substantially equal to that given her nonhandicapped classmates."[15] The Court clearly felt that the total package of services furnished to Amy by the school board was reasonably calculated to enable her to benefit from the education.

How does one determine whether the benefit conferred is enough to be appropriate? Clearly, the Supreme Court rejected the circuit court standard that potential had to be maximized, so how do we quantify the *Rowley* standard? The Court stated that for a child like Amy, who is being educated in a regular classroom in a public school system, "the system itself monitors the educational progress of the child" and "the grading and advancement system thus constitutes an important factor in determining educational benefit."[16]

Is that all? A quick reading of *Rowley* might seem to suggest that the standard for judging appropriateness is whether the child passes each year. For more highly functioning students with disabilities, who work extremely hard and scrape by, a "passing grades" standard would seem to leave parents no argument for any special services at all, let alone increased levels of service. One could almost hear a school administrator telling a parent, "Your child's passing grades mean that the disability has no adverse effect on educational performance, and thus your child is not even qualified for special education." The lower courts had found that Amy's "energy and eagerness" were not spent in achievement but rather were used to compensate for her disability. Shouldn't a program that meets a child's unique needs offer more than just an opportunity to scrape by, burn out, and be socially promoted?

*Rowley* is much stronger than that. First, *Rowley* says that "the grading system" (not just passing grades) is "an important factor"[17] (not the only factor). Second, the passing grades factor would apply only to students whose curricular offerings "approximate the grade levels used in the State's regular education."[18] Children whose instruction deviates noticeably from the regular offering would have to be judged differently. Third, if a school were to say instruction must have been appropriate because a child passed, then courts would scrutinize the honesty of the grades and the annual promotion. The Court stated that "children who graduate from our public school systems are considered by our society to have been educated at least to the grade level they have completed."[19] Fourth, the passing grades factor is more likely to be judged in the negative: A child with a disability who receives regular instruction but does not receive a passing grade must therefore not have received an appropriate education. Finally, passing is a measure applicable only to instruction. The appropriateness of related services must still be determined with IEP-relevant criteria. One must not forget that Amy Rowley received, and was entitled to, more than just instruction in a regular classroom. She received 1 hour per day of tutoring. The IEP plan had to reflect the goal of providing that service and to specify its frequency (daily), its duration (an hour each day), and the qualifications of the service provider (a certified teacher of the deaf). Amy also received speech therapy. Her need for that service was translated into a frequency of three times weekly with a duration of 1 hour per session. Further, the speech therapist would have to meet state standards.

Thus, whether Amy Rowley passed was not the only question being asked about her education. The real standard, inherent in the entirety of the EHA and consistent with the majority opinion in *Rowley*, was whether the individual child was meeting her individual goal as stated in her individual IEP plan.

The Supreme Court refers to the IEP plan as a "written record of reasonable expectations."[20] Thus, the following questions form the criteria for setting up the appropriateness determination: What are reasonable expectations for the child's performance this year, based on individual learning capacity? And what program (specially designed instruction tailored to the unique needs of the student, plus related services without which the child could not benefit from the specially designed instruction) is needed to enable the child to reach that reasonable goal?

A reasonable expectation for Amy Rowley was surely more than just the barest benefit. If it had been "appropriate" for her just to scrape by, then she would not have been entitled to 5 hours of tutoring and 3 hours of speech therapy each week, plus an FM hearing aid.

Who sets the reasonable expectations? The IEP meeting is the decision-making forum. The Supreme Court recognized the IEP process as part of an appropriate education, stating, "It seems to us no exaggeration to say that Congress placed every bit as much emphasis upon compliance with procedures giving parents a large measure of participation at every stage of the administrative process as it did upon the measurement of the resulting IEP against a substantive standard."[21]

Thus, the question whether there is an appropriate educational offering has two parts: one substantive (Does it confer benefit that is reasonable, given the child's learning capacity?) and one procedural (Were all procedures followed, especially those that involve parents as participants in the process?).

The Supreme Court emphasized the congressional view of the importance of parental participation, recognizing "Congress' effort to maximize parental involvement in the education of each handicapped child."[22] The Court also noted that "Congress sought to protect individual children by providing for parental involvement . . . in the formulation of the child's individual education program" and that "the primary responsibility . . . for choosing the educational method most suitable to the child's needs was left by the EHA to state and local educational agencies in cooperation with the parents or guardians of the child."[23]

The Supreme Court pointed out that each educational agency was required under the EHA to have a written, comprehensive system of personnel development by which it would "acquire and disseminate" what Congress called "promising educational practices."[24] It was the Supreme Court's understanding that, given such a plan, the educational agency would have available a full range of options to discuss with the parents about educational approaches and methodology. Then the IEP team, including the parents, would choose "the method most suitable to the child's needs."[25]

Thus, after *Rowley,* a complaint from parents that they were left out of the process would be seriously scrutinized by the courts. A complaint that parental information about the child's unique needs was ignored, or that the parents' input about reasonable expectations based upon their child's learning capacity was not solicited, would suggest fatal procedural flaws. Similarly, a complaint that the school district did not choose methodology from an array of promising educational practices but simply offered the one and only program currently at its disposal would suggest a violation of *Rowley.*

Therefore, *Rowley* has left us with a substantive standard and a procedural standard. Substantively, appropriateness means that the program is (a) related to the child's learning capacity, (b) specially designed for the child's unique needs and not merely what is offered to others, and (c) calculated to confer educational benefit. In addition, all procedures prescribed in the Act must be followed, especially those involving parents as equal partners in the process.

Ironically, Amy "lost" at the Supreme Court level because she did not get the sign language interpreter she requested. But everyone else "won" by getting a fair and workable explanation of what constitutes an appropriate educational offering.

## Notes

1. 458 U.S. 176 (1982).
2. 632 F.2d 945 (2nd Cir. 1980).
3. 483 F.Supp. 528 (S.D. NY 1980).
4. 476 F.Supp. 583 (E.D. PA 1979).
5. Notes 2 and 3, supra.
6. Rowley, note 1, supra.
7. 334 F.Supp. 1257 (E.D. PA 1971).
8. 405 F.Supp. 946 (E.D. PA 1975).
9. 419 F.Supp. 960 (E.D. PA 1976).
10. Rowley, note 1, supra, at 191.
11. Rowley, at 198–199.
12. Rowley, at 181.
13. Rowley, at 200.
14. Rowley, at 206–207.
15. Rowley, at 211.
16. Rowley, at 203.
17. Rowley, at 203.
18. Rowley, at 203.
19. Rowley, at 203.
20. Rowley, at 209.
21. Rowley, at 205–206.
22. Rowley, at 182, note 6.
23. Rowley, at 207.
24. Rowley, at 207.
25. Rowley, at 207.

# Programs Specially Designed to Meet Unique Needs

At the time that federal special education laws were passed, every school district in the United States had some kind of ongoing special education program. Congress recognized, however, that an estimated 1 million young people with disabilities were being excluded entirely from any contact with public schools. Many public school officials testified to Congress that they just did not know how to serve those youngsters or, in some cases, did not believe that those children's needs should have to be met by a public school. Further, an estimated half of the remaining 4 million youngsters with disabilities were receiving inappropriate education. Congress found that they were put in classes designed for other students and were just left there to fend for themselves, waiting to drop out of school.

It made sense, then, that if the schools were to start serving a million children they said they did not know how to serve, and if they were going to make programs appropriate for another 2 million, fundamental changes were needed.

The solution Congress required was that programs be specially designed. As the Supreme Court had found in *Rowley*, Congress intended for programs to be *individualized, personalized, tailored,* and *specially designed* to meet the unique needs of the particular child. The Supreme Court also stated in *Rowley* that the IEP committee was to choose the methodology *most suited* to the child's unique needs.

The realization underlying the legislation and reflected in the court findings was that children are different. A program not specially designed for a given child might have no benefit; worse, it could cause harm. That was the problem facing Chuck's parents. The school was proposing a program that they were convinced would hurt their child, perhaps irreparably.

When Chuck was 2 years old he had meningitis, and a hearing impairment resulted. Because his impairment came so early in life, he had a severe delay in developing speech. His parents located a private program at the Houston School for Deaf Children and started him there immediately. Chuck wore hearing aids and had some residual hearing. The private school's evaluations showed that he was a good candidate for its "oral" program.

The oral approach was geared to the acquisition of speech skills to the fullest extent possible. The school's motto was "Our students speak for themselves." No exposure to sign language was allowed because of the school's belief that it interfered with the development of speech. The private school teachers were not opposed to sign language for children who needed it, but where there was an opportunity to develop speech and move into the mainstream, they fought for the oral approach.

The private school's goal was for its students to function successfully enough to proceed into public schools. The school officials thus informed Chuck's parents of their rights under the Education of the Handicapped Act (EHA) when he was about to turn 3. Chuck's parents had never received any such information from their local public school, so when they learned of their rights, they asked for a meeting with the public school to discuss programming.

At that meeting, the school district representatives explained how they educated children with hearing impairments. The state operated a regional program for students with hearing impairments, which had one site in the school district. Chuck would attend that program. The program's approach, called the "total communication" approach, emphasized sign language, with no speech therapy and no attempt to develop speech.

I have had clients in total communication programs that actually *were* total, fostering one child's oral ability, another's lipreading, and still another's sign language. (A good total communication teacher is amazing to watch.) The children attended those programs for only part of the school day, according to their needs. They spent the rest of the day with nondisabled students. However, personnel at Chuck's private school had stories of former students who had entered public school programs with a so-called total communication approach, which really consisted only of sign language. Those students had become sign language dependent, had lost the ability to speak, and had become segregated in programs for students with hearing impairments rather than being integrated into the life of the school.

Although the meeting with school officials did not produce a written IEP plan for Chuck, the parents felt they had heard enough to clearly reject the school district's idea. There had been no evaluation of Chuck's unique needs and abilities. There was no attempt even to consider developing his speech.

The first time I met Chuck at the private school, we had an active conversation. As he left the room I heard another student ask him who I was. Chuck very distinctly said, "I think he's my new doctor." It seemed ridiculous not to continue to develop his speech. Worse, it was illegal. The EHA did not intend placing children in one-size-fits-all programs regardless of their needs and abilities. It required programs to be specially designed to meet unique needs.

The practical problem for the school district was that there was no alternative to the state-run day program. School officials assumed that whatever the state had ordained was appropriate. More important, the funding reimbursement schedule was tied to that program, leaving the local school with no extra funds. If the plan were for Chuck to attend his home school rather than the state-run program, we were not sure whether speech therapy assistance would even be available.

In our contact with the state education agency over this issue, it was clear that the state strongly opposed hearing-impaired students' attending their home schools and causing any resources to be reallocated to those home schools. A child like Chuck could unravel the entire state plan for educating students with hearing impairments. I knew of some such students who were in fact at their home schools, but they were told that, in choosing the home school, they waived any related services.

Chuck's parents asked for a hearing to contest the school decision that nothing other than sign language would be offered. The hearing officer assigned, who happened to be a speech pathologist, made a thorough review of Chuck's clinical and educational history and concluded that the appropriate educational offering was for Chuck to continue at the private school with the public school paying the bill.

The school district disagreed with the hearing officer's decision, but rather than appealing it, the school board voted to set it aside and reinstate the school's IEP plan. Would the state enforce the hearing officer's decision? What were the parents' rights?

It was obvious that the state had to be a major defendant in our lawsuit. The state had set up the one-size-fits-all approach to students with hearing impairments. The state had set up the funding formula that discouraged local schools from developing local programs. The state had set up an administrative hearing system that was illegal. And now the state would not even inform Chuck's parents about their procedural rights.

One of the procedural issues the parents had complained about was a lack of notice. Before their first meeting with the local school district, they were entitled to written notice explaining what the school was proposing.[1] Not knowing what the school had in mind (i.e., automatic placement at a regional day program with a total communication approach), Chuck's parents were ill equipped to argue their case in that meeting.

The parents wanted to appeal that decision and asked for written notice of the procedures. That request was denied. They asked for and received a hearing, which they won. Then the school had the hearing results reversed in a procedure unknown to the parents. The parents were told they could have another hearing. They asked for an explanation of their rights in that hearing and were refused.

I appeared at the second hearing to make two motions that would bring the state board of education clearly into the picture as a defendant. The hearing officer, an experienced attorney, quickly understood what we were doing and denied our motions so that we could appeal.

When Chuck's case was finally decided in federal court,[2] the court stated "that the Defendants created a procedural quagmire of Kafkaesque proportions which effectively denied the Plaintiffs their right to a fair opportunity to present their complaints regarding Charles' educational placement." The court ruled that "the failure of the local Defendants to provide the Plaintiffs with written prior notice of all available procedural safeguards and of their rights regarding an appropriate free public education for Charles violated the EAHCA [Education for All Handicapped Children Act]."[3]

Six years elapsed from the time the case was filed in federal court until the time it was concluded. In the meantime, Chuck stayed at the private placement and continued to develop his oral ability to the point that he would barely need any related services to succeed in a mainstream placement. At the end of the second year, the public school suggested another IEP meeting. The lawyers attended that meeting because the subject matter was in litigation.

The local school announced that it was creating an oral program at Chuck's neighborhood school and recommended that program as the appropriate placement for Chuck. The parents agreed, but because the school year was ending, it was agreed that Chuck would finish at the private school. During the summer Chuck's father was transferred out of state, and Chuck never enrolled in the oral program that had been developed because of him.

The case continued, however, because Chuck's parents had been paying for the private school. They wanted to be reimbursed for the costs incurred from the time the public school made the inappropriate placement recommendation of the sign language program until the time the proper IEP plan was proposed. We also wanted to be reimbursed for our attorneys' fees.

Years later we went to trial. Our strongest evidence on the substantive side of the case was the fact that the school district had finally started to offer the oral approach that we had requested. We had wanted a program specially designed to meet Chuck's unique needs. Once appropriate attention had been paid to his unique oral ability, the only specially designed program that made sense was an oral approach. The court agreed: "Moreover, the tardy initiation of an oral approach program underscores the Plaintiff's contention that Charles was entitled to this free appropriate educational program *ab initio.*"[4]

From a procedural standpoint, we could show the illegal procedures used by the defendants. After we had filed the case, I went to Washington, D.C., and met with federal officials. We sent them copies of our pleadings and kept them apprised of the case. We asked that they withhold federal funds until the illegal procedures were stopped. In our discovery phase of the case we obtained all the correspondence between the federal officials and the state education agency, and funds were indeed withheld over this issue. The court found that "the unduly elaborate procedures employed by the Defendants manifestly violated the purposes and spirit of the EAHCA by impeding and discouraging parental attempts to obtain an appropriate public education for handicapped children."[5]

Every case has a soap opera dimension. Our weak spot was that, after our fight to get an oral approach for Chuck, he never enrolled. That was certainly not his fault: His family moved out of state. But if the local school could convince the court that we had not been sincere in our fight for an appropriate public school program, it might hurt us. One school official had been quoted as saying that the parents just wanted a free ride at the private school.

If that had been true, then the parents' initial rejection of the public school program would not have been very relevant. According to that theory, it did not matter what the public school had offered; the parents would have rejected it. Some courts had held that the school should not be penalized for a less-than-appropriate offering if the parents would have rejected the offering in any case.

We wanted to avoid such a finding. Our real "proof" was in the later IEP meeting, where the local school first offered the oral approach we had been seeking. Our position was that we had accepted that approach. The local school's position had become that we had never accepted that offer of an oral approach, demonstrating that we only wanted a private school for Chuck and would never consider a public program.

The public school had audiotaped that IEP meeting. We asked for a copy of the tape and were told it could not be found. We subpoenaed it through the court; the school replied that it no longer existed. At trial it became obvious during the testimony of one defendant that school officials must have listened to the tape very recently. Upon questioning they admitted that the tape had been found but that, rather than being produced as ordered, it had been destroyed. The soap opera suddenly turned in our favor. We knew that the tape supported our position, and now the court would have to assume that, too.

The court ordered the public school to reimburse Chuck's parents for the costs of the private school from the date of the inappropriate offering until the date of the appropriate offering. We felt that the real victory could be claimed if some youngster with an oral ability whom we had never even met benefited because Chuck had caused his school to meet the unique needs of a child with a hearing impairment.

## Notes

1. 34 C.F.R. 300.504, 505.
2. Hopkins v. Aldine Independent School District and State Department of Education, EHLR 555:412 (S.D. TX 1984).
3. Hopkins, at 415.
4. Hopkins, at 415.
5. Hopkins, at 415.

# Related Services

When a case is begun, no one knows how long it will take or how far it will go through the system before the issues are resolved. When the Tatros asked for their daughter to be catheterized by public school personnel, they never imagined that the matter would go to the United States Supreme Court, require testimony to Congress and an amendment to the Education of the Handicapped Act (EHA), and take a total of 10 years and 3 months to conclude.

Amber was born with spina bifida, a condition that caused her to need a catheter to empty her bladder. At the age of 3, when she first qualified for services from her local public school, Amber was unable to self-catheterize and needed help. Her doctor had prescribed the times of day at which she was to be catheterized, and one of those times fell during school hours. When Amber's parents approached the public school officials to arrange for her program, they requested that someone at the school accompany Amber to the bathroom and assist with catheterization.

The school officials refused, arguing that catheterization was a medical procedure. They said that the fact that the procedure required a physician's prescription made it a medical treatment and thus placed it outside the requirements of the EHA. The EHA, they held, had clearly distinguished between medical diagnostic services (required at public expense when needed for a student's programming) and medical treatment (not considered a requirement of the Act because it was unduly burdensome and beyond the competence of school systems).[1]

Further complicating the problem, the school reportedly relied on the previous experience of a board member who insisted that catheterization required expensive sterile procedures. Sterile catheterization would have required the purchase and maintenance of machinery to be kept in the school building. Raising the specter of liability, the school district thought sterile catheterization was risky and could cause serious injury to the child.

Amber's parents pointed out that the catheterization required by their physician was not the sterile catheterization of the 1960s but rather clean, intermittent catheterization. The latter, now recognized by the American Academy of Pediatrics, required only washing one's hands with soap and water, was not risky, and did not require the involvement of a physician. It could be taught to any school person in a matter of minutes.

The school remained steadfast: No school person would be allowed to perform catheterization. The practical result was that Amber would be barred from school. She simply could not attend school without catheterization any more than other students could attend if they were not permitted to use the restroom.

The school offered two alternatives. Amber could go to school and not receive catheterization, or she could remain at home full time and be taught homebound until she was old enough to self-catheterize. Years of homebound isolation seemed ridiculous: Amber had every right to be in public school and interact with other children. Because Amber could not be served in her home school, her parents placed her in a private school that provided not only educational services but also the simple related service of catheterization.

Amber's parents believed in trying to settle problems locally, so they asked to address the school board in the hope that the board would correct the situation. The board, however, still apparently believed that catheterization was a risky and expensive procedure. The parents felt they had no alternative but to hire a lawyer and proceed to an impartial hearing, which they won. However, the state board of education illegally overturned that decision, and the Tatros had to appeal into federal court.

During this time I received a call from the federal special education office in Washington, D.C., asking why this matter had not been sent there as a complaint. It was so clear-cut, the federal officials insisted, that they would have ordered the state to see that the procedure was provided. I invited them to do so; however, they replied that, now that the courts were involved, they had to stay out of it.

The parents appealed the state board decision into federal district court, asking for a preliminary injunction ordering the school to provide the catheterization service. They had raised issues under both the EHA and Section 504 of the Rehabilitation Act. They argued that the Acts required such a procedure as a related service and that failure to provide it created an access issue, barring their daughter from school as if the door had been slammed in her face. The school argued that catheterization was not a related service because it did not arise out of the need to educate Amber. They argued that she was cognitively able to receive benefit in her academic subjects and that catheterization thus was unrelated to education.

The district court ruled against the parents; it just did not believe that Congress intended for schools to involve themselves in a procedure such as catheterization. The court also ruled that Section 504 did not require "the setting up of governmental health care for people seeking to participate" in federally funded programs.[2]

The parents received a great deal of support from the community, which, according to newspaper articles and editorials, was disturbed that the public school was spending its dollars to avoid providing such a simple service. Special education directors in adjoining school districts had made clear that they provided catheterization services in their districts. Everyone wondered why this school district did not consider its staff competent to do what adjacent districts were doing so easily.

The parents appealed the decision to the Fifth Circuit Court of Appeals, which quickly reversed the district court decision and clearly upheld the student's right to receive services like catheterization during the school day. First, it held that clean, intermittent catheterization (CIC) was a related service under the EHA because, without the procedure, Amber could not attend class and benefit from special education. Second, the Fifth Circuit found that the school district's refusal to provide catheterization excluded Amber from a federally funded educational program in violation of Section 504 of the Rehabilitation Act.[3]

Because the hearing in district court had simply been on a preliminary injunction, the Fifth Circuit sent the case back to the district court to develop a full factual record and apply the legal principles stated by the circuit court. Further, the Fifth Circuit remanded the decision back to the district court for a hearing on an award of attorneys' fees and damages to the parents for the costs of private schooling.

At the district court the school district renewed its arguments. It claimed that related services under the EHA mentioned medical diagnostic services and that, therefore, medical services could be considered related services only if they were for evaluation purposes. The school insisted that catheterization was a medical service because it was provided pursuant to a physician's prescription.

The parents countered that the EHA also provided for school health services as related services and that several other related services, such as physical therapy, also required a physician's prescription but were not considered medical. The school continued to argue that a physician was needed to provide catheterization and that, if this service were required of public schools, then kidney dialysis would follow.

The district court, ruling within the straitjacket imposed by the Fifth Circuit, found for the parents.[4] The Texas Medical Association had entered the case as an amicus curiae to explain that, under Texas law, a nurse or other qualified person might administer CIC, without engaging in the practice of medicine, even though a doctor had prescribed the procedure. The district court held that, because a doctor was not needed to administer the procedure, the procedure was not a medical service under the EHA. This was a very important ruling because several other states insisted that physical and occupational therapy were also excludable "medical" services. The district court ruling made clear that a physician's involvement did not excuse school districts from providing catheterization, physical therapy, or occupational therapy.

The court then found catheterization to be a related service under the EHA and ordered the school district to modify Amber's IEP plan to include catheterization during school hours. It also awarded compensatory damages against the school district and the state to reimburse Amber's parents for the costs of procuring private services.

The district court also held that the school district and the state had violated Section 504 of the Rehabilitation Act. Because that Act specifically allowed an award of attorneys' fees, the district court found the parents to be prevailing parties and awarded attorneys' fees against the school district and the state board of education.[5]

The school district still insisted that it was right and appealed the decision back to the Fifth Circuit Court of Appeals. That court affirmed the district court's decision that catheterization was not a medical service, that compensatory relief was available under the EHA, and that attorneys' fees should be awarded under the Rehabilitation Act.[6]

Still dissatisfied, the school district appealed to the United States Supreme Court. A very similar case, *Tokarcik v. Forest Hills*,[7] had dealt specifically with the issue of catheterization and had produced a result quite similar to the Fifth Circuit's decision. That case had also been appealed to the Supreme Court, which had declined to review it. Now, suddenly, in the *Tatro* case, the Supreme Court saw something different that it wanted to review.

As we worked on the brief, we all speculated on what difference between the two cases had led the Supreme Court to want to hear this one. What were we missing? What was of sufficient interest in *Tatro* that enough justices had voted to hear the case? Did they want to silence the argument of school districts like this one by making the obligation clear for the entire nation? Or did the justices want to take the case to reverse it for the entire nation? We studied the *Tokarcik* and *Tatro* petitions for certiorari (the brief that asks the Court to hear the case), trying to divine the answer, but we never could.

When the time came for oral argument, 9-year-old Amber and her family attended the proceedings in Washington. Amber, who walks with the aid of leg braces, discovered that the Supreme Court was not readily accessible. She was told she could enter from the rear and take a service elevator up to the level of the courtroom, but she preferred to walk up the long steps in front. When she arrived at the top, a newspaper photographer took her picture in front of the Court. I am proud to have that picture hanging above my desk.

There were two simple questions before the Supreme Court: first, whether catheterization was a related service required under the Acts and, second, whether it was excluded as a medical treatment.[8] The school district sought to prevent the Supreme Court from pursuing this line of inquiry, quoting the Court's decision in *Rowley*.[9] The school district argued that a court could only ask whether the school had followed the EHA's procedural requirements and that, because the school did have an IEP plan in place, the court could inquire no further. The Supreme Court made clear that courts could indeed go further and that judicial review was appropriate in such cases as this to determine whether the school had met both the law's procedural requirements and the school's substantive obligations.[10]

The Supreme Court found clearly that catheterization was a supportive service that fit under the definition of related services. Such related services are intended to enable a child to benefit from special education, and it was clear that, without catheterization available during the school day, Amber could not attend school.[11]

The Supreme Court saw the issue as one of access, as the parents had urged. In the view of the Court, Congress had been concerned that public education be made available to children with disabilities and that such access be meaningful:[12]

> A service that enables a handicapped child to remain at school during the day is an important means of providing students with the meaningful access to education that Congress envisioned. The Act makes specific provision for services, like transportation, for example, that do no more than enable a child to be physically present in class. . . . Services like CIC that permit a child to remain at school during the day are no less related to the effort to educate than are services that enable the child to reach, enter, or exit the school.[13]

The Court thus defined the relationship of a "related service" to the offering of some specially designed instruction: The related service is related to the offering of education *in general.* The school had argued that, because Amber's need for catheterization did not cause a modification in the way core academic subjects were offered, that particular service was not related to instruction. But the Supreme Court made clear that services needed to reach, enter, exit, or remain in school during the day are related to the offering of education and as such are essential related services.[14]

Next the Court turned to the more difficult issue of whether catheterization is a medical service that is beyond the expectations of the Act. The Court began by pointing out that regulations defining related services specify the inclusion of "school health services," which are in turn defined as "services provided by a qualified school nurse or other qualified person." "Medical services," in contrast, are defined as "services provided by a licensed physician."[15]

The Supreme Court wondered what Congress had in mind when it created a distinction between medical and other related services. Because Congress had not elaborated on the issue, the Court looked at the next source of interpretation: the administrative body that had promulgated the regulations, the Department of Education. The Supreme Court said that those regulations were entitled to deference. The Court found that the Department of Education "concluded that [the distinction] was designed to spare schools from an obligation to provide a service that might well prove unduly expensive and beyond the range of their competence."[16]

The Court further said:

> School nurses have long been a part of the educational system, and the Secretary [of Education] could therefore reasonably conclude that school nursing services are not the sort of burden that Congress intended to exclude as a "medical service." By limiting the "medical service" exclusion to the services of a physician or hospital, both far more expensive, the Secretary has given a permissible construction to the provision.[17]

Thus, the line was drawn at services requiring a physician or a hospital, and school nursing services were to be provided.

The school district was still claiming, "Catheterization today, kidney dialysis tomorrow."[18] The Supreme Court attempted to assuage the district's fears:

> To keep in perspective the obligation to provide services that relate to the health and educational needs of handicapped students, we note several limitations that should minimize the burden petitioners fear. First, to be entitled

to related services, a child must be handicapped so as to require special education. . . . Second, only those services necessary to aid a handicapped child to benefit from special education must be provided, regardless how easily a school nurse or a layperson could furnish them. For example, if a particular medication or treatment may appropriately be administered to a handicapped child other than during the school day, a school is not required to provide nursing services to administer it. Third, the regulations state that school nursing services must be provided only if they can be performed by a nurse or other qualified person, not if they must be performed by a physician.[19]

Thus, the Court had set up a simple standard: The child must be handicapped; the child must receive the services during the school day or otherwise be barred from receiving an education; and the services can be provided by someone with less training than a physician.

The school district was still worried about liability, and the Supreme Court addressed that concern very curtly in a footnote:

The introduction of handicapped children into a school creates numerous possibilities for injury and liability. . . . Congress assumed that states receiving the generous grants under the Act were up to the job of managing these new risks. Whether [the school district] decides to purchase more liability insurance or to persuade the state to extend the limitation on liability, the risks posed by CIC should not prove to be a large burden.[20]

The Supreme Court then added two sentences that caused years of argument. The school district, mistaking the type of catheterization required as sterile rather than CIC, had argued that the parents were asking the school to purchase and maintain expensive equipment. But the parents sent Amber to school each day with her catheter, and absolutely no equipment was required. The Court simply observed, "We note that respondents are not asking petitioner to provide equipment that Amber needs for CIC. They seek only the services of a qualified person at the school."[21]

This led some school districts to insist that the Supreme Court had ordered schools not to provide equipment. Obviously, whenever the school had to provide the service, it would have to provide the qualified person and the equipment or contract for their provision.

The final paragraph in the Supreme Court decision dropped a bomb. The Court had decided, on the same day as the *Tatro* decision, the case of *Smith v. Robinson*,[22] finding that parents litigating under special education statutes could not receive attorneys' fees because the EHA did not provide for such awards. Even though Section 504 of the Rehabilitation Act does allow such awards, the Supreme Court announced that parents must first exhaust all their claims under the EHA. If they are successful solely under the EHA, then they cannot raise Section 504. Consequently, parents in that situation would "win" only under the EHA, legislation that does not provide for attorneys' fees.

Amber's parents were shocked, as were their attorneys. The attorneys had taken the case on a contingency basis, not charging the clients directly but expecting to be paid from the other side when the parents prevailed. After 6 years, having won on all the important issues 9 to 0 in the Supreme Court, they could not believe they were not entitled to attorneys' fees. The school district had never argued, during the entire case, that the prevailing party would *not* be able to receive attorneys' fees. The district court and the Fifth Circuit had both said that the parents, as prevailing parties, were entitled to attorneys' fees. The issue was not raised at any judicial level and was not briefed or addressed. It was not a subject of review by the Supreme Court and was not argued before that Court.

How in the world could parents be expected to bear the expense of attorneys' fees—from a hearing, to review at the state level, to review by the state board of education, to rehearing by the state board, to federal district court, to the circuit court of appeals, back to the district court, back to the circuit court, and finally to the United States Supreme Court—if they could not count on reimbursement of those fees if they were the prevailing party?

The Tatros would not have begun the lawsuit had they known that it exposed them to great expense and offered no chance to recover any of their costs. And what attorney would ever consider taking such a case on a contingency? Attorneys would have to charge as they went along, and only very rich parents could afford to invoke the protections of the EHA.

Thus, in the midst of an incredible victory, which affected schoolchildren all across the United States, Amber's parents felt they had been dealt a terrible blow. But, characteristic of this family, they did not let the story stop there. Justice Brennan, who agreed with the other justices on the issue of catheterization, dissented on the issue of attorneys' fees and had said, in his dissent in *Smith*, that "Congress will now have to revisit the matter."[23]

The Tatros helped Congress "revisit" the issue and eventually won their attorney fee award. That story is told in chapter 12.

# Notes

1. Irving Independent School District v. Tatro (hereinafter Tatro), 468 U.S. 883 (1984), at 892.
2. Tatro v. Texas, 481 F.Supp. 1224 (N.D. TX 1979).
3. Tatro v. Texas, 625 F.2d 557 (5th Cir. 1980).
4. Tatro v. Texas, 516 F.Supp. 968 (N.D. TX 1981).
5. Tatro v. Texas, note 4, supra.
6. Tatro v. Texas, 703 F.2d 823 (5th Cir. 1983).
7. 665 F.2d 443 (3rd Cir. 1981).
8. Tatro, note 1, supra, at 890.
9. 458 U.S. 176 (1981).
10. Tatro, note 1, supra, at 890, note 6.
11. Tatro, at 890.
12. Tatro, at 891.
13. Tatro, at 891.
14. Tatro, at 891.
15. Tatro, at 892.
16. Tatro, at 892.
17. Tatro, at 893.
18. We had never taken this seriously, but we could not afford the chance that the Court would treat it seriously and ask a question during oral argument. Consequently, we had an excellent memorandum prepared by a nursing law expert, Dr. Darlene A. Martin, of the University of Texas School of Nursing at Galveston. It explained in detail the differences between procedures that might be required of a school nurse or other qualified person and procedures like dialysis that would necessarily involve a physician.
19. Tatro, at 894.
20. Tatro, at 893, note 12.
21. Tatro, at 895.
22. 468 U.S. 992 (1984).
23. Smith, note 22, supra.

# Least Restrictive Environment

Danny was born with a great advantage. He has a wonderful and supportive family who include him in every aspect of their lives. Danny was also born with Down syndrome and, as a result, has some degree of retardation. By the time he was 3 years old and ready for preschool programs he also had a delay in developing speech.

When Danny's parents approached their public school district, they were informed of an early childhood class that provided 2 hours and 45 minutes per day of programming. Danny entered the class and did very well. By all reports, the teacher was exceptionally good. In some ways, Danny was the star of the class. The school had tested his IQ, which was so high that the school had classified him as having "borderline retardation."

But Danny's parents felt that one thing was missing in his education. The early childhood class included only students with disabilities. They felt that Danny needed to be around nondisabled children as well so that he could work on developing language and behavior. They felt that he could also benefit from a longer school day because he had previously been in a private school with a full day.

In the spring the school held an IEP meeting for Danny. The school proposal was that Danny continue another year in the early childhood class. Under that plan, Danny would again be in a class of youngsters with disabilities, and he would have a short school day. His parents pressed for more, but the only option the school could offer was to let Danny attend the prekindergarten class as well as the early childhood class. School personnel cautioned the parents that the prekindergarten class was for nondisabled children and that, in their view, Danny could not benefit from the curriculum. They further warned Danny's parents that the teacher hired for that class was young and had never taught a child with a disability.

The parents knew that some modifications would be required to meet Danny's particular needs if he were to benefit from the prekindergarten class, and they assumed that any such modifications could be worked out in the IEP meeting. But the school personnel said no. Apparently, the school position was that an IEP plan was to be written by the special education staff only for special education services delivered in a special education class. An IEP plan could not be drawn up for services in a regular education class. Further, the school held that the teacher was a "regular" teacher and could not, therefore, be governed by an IEP plan written by the special education staff.

The parents' real concern was for Danny to have exposure to nondisabled students, so they felt that the prekindergarten class was worth a try. Because Danny would now attend prekindergarten in the morning and the early childhood class in the afternoon, he would be staying at school for lunch as well. His parents hoped the lunchroom experience would provide further opportunity for interactions with nondisabled students. But for that lunchroom time to be beneficial, Danny needed some help. Not only had he never gone through a lunch line before, he had no friends in the lunchroom. The program was not at his home school; it was far out of his neighborhood. The parents hoped to arrange for a buddy to smooth Danny's entrance into this new environment.

The school position was that lunch, like prekindergarten, was regular education and that only students who were ready for it should participate. If Danny needed special help, then he should not be there, so no buddy would be arranged. At the end of the IEP meeting the plan was for Danny to attend prekindergarten daily, with no modifications in the class; go to lunch alone in the regular cafeteria; and attend the early childhood class.

Danny's mother contacted the prekindergarten teacher to offer some information about Danny. She gave the teacher a book about Down syndrome and told her about an upcoming conference that would deal with related educational issues. She also suggested that the prekindergarten teacher talk with the early childhood teacher about Danny and about what the teachers would be doing in the two classes. But when school started, the prekindergarten teacher had not read the book, attended any conferences, or talked to the other teacher.

The school year did not start out well for Danny. Although the special education early childhood class was going as well as expected and Danny was continuing to progress, school personnel let it be known almost from the beginning that they did not believe Danny belonged in the prekindergarten class. According to them, he was not participating and his lack of participation was disruptive. They reported that Danny would scribble on a piece of paper while other students painstakingly copied an assignment from the board. He would climb under his desk. He would occasionally put his hands over his ears. And he seemed to be developing a stutter, which the school personnel thought might be an emotional reaction to being in a class that was too difficult for him.

Danny's lunchroom experience was also unsatisfactory. The teachers thought he was not getting an appropriate diet. He was not interacting with other children. He was seen crawling under the table, which, they felt, indicated that he was trying to get away from everyone.

Danny's mother visited the prekindergarten class to observe her son. She made suggestions to the teacher on possible modifications to Danny's curriculum, even though the teacher had said that she did not want to make any more changes. The one modification she had made, at the suggestion of a teacher she knew in another district, was to get large-handled scissors and large crayons.

The dispute over whether Danny belonged in the prekindergarten class reached an impasse in October. Danny's mother observed the class working on an assignment in which the teacher drew on the board an astronaut composed of circles and triangles and the students dutifully copied it at their desks. Once the drawing was copied, a discussion of the concepts *same* and *different* would begin. Danny quickly lost interest. Danny's mother suggested that someone could draw a large and small circle and a large and small triangle on Danny's paper, and he could just color them. Then he could participate in the discussion of same and different. That struck the teacher as too great a modification of the assignment, and she refused.

Shortly thereafter, the school asked Danny's mother to attend a meeting. When she arrived, she discovered that it was an IEP meeting. The school presented her with the decision, already made, that Danny was to be removed from the prekindergarten class as well as from lunch and recess with the nondisabled students. The school position was clear: that Danny could come to school only for the early childhood special education class.

Danny's mother protested, insisting that Danny had to have some contact with nondisabled students so that he could continue to develop his speech and behavior. The school offered a counterproposal: Danny could come to lunch three times a week, but only if his mother accompanied him the entire time, and Danny could play at recess with the other students. However, because Danny would be at school only during the early childhood special education class, the daily half-hour recess with nondisabled students would be taken out of the early childhood class time.

For Danny's mother, that was no solution. If she were standing by Danny at lunch, could he have social interaction with other children? If Danny left early childhood each day for a half hour to play with a group of children whom he did not know, would there be social interaction, or would Danny feel left out? Would his social development progress or regress under the school's proposal? And because the only place where everyone agreed that Danny was achieving was in the early childhood class, would cutting 2½ hours per week out of that instruction be the right thing for him?

Danny's parents rejected the school proposal and asked for a hearing before an impartial due process hearing officer. Assigned to their case was a new hearing officer who had just left his job in the state education agency, where he had been in the office of general counsel and had been in charge of special education. He had written many of the regulations that Danny's parents would be arguing about. They asked the hearing officer to withdraw and be replaced by someone with no such interest in the case, but the hearing officer refused.

After a lengthy hearing that lasted 5 days and produced a transcript of over 2500 pages, the hearing officer found completely for the school district. He wrote that Danny's behavior showed that he was being harmed in the prekindergarten class. The hearing officer found that Danny functioned at a level so low that he could not master the curriculum designed for that class and that he therefore did not belong in the class. He found further that Danny required 100 percent of the teacher's time and 100 percent of the aide's time and that this was disruptive to the other students in the class. Finally, the hearing officer told Danny's parents that their priorities were wrong and that they were obviously willing to hurt their son to promote their misguided notion of mainstreaming.

Danny's parents appealed to the federal district court and asked me to help in the case. We argued first that Danny actually performed better than the hearing officer had indicated. Part of Danny's problem, we pointed out, was caused by the school's refusal to obey the law and draft an IEP plan that dealt with his needs in the regular class. We quoted the opinion of Justice Rehnquist in *Rowley* that handicapped students would not be receiving appropriate education if they were "left to fend for themselves in classrooms designed for education of their nonhandicapped peers."[1]

One anecdote really stood out. Danny's regular prekindergarten teacher testified at the hearing that Danny was failing to benefit, citing as an example the fact that he did not interact socially. When Danny would complete work, this teacher said, he would not show it to other students. The implication was that he was withdrawn. Danny's special education teacher, however, testified that in her class she discouraged

Danny from showing his completed work to others because she kept all the students on task. Thus, Danny was not doing something that was required in regular education because he would be punished for it in special education. But the school had not bothered to put this information together.

Second, we argued that the IEP plan *could* address activities in the regular classroom environment, including lunch and recess, and that the regular teacher should have attended Danny's IEP meeting. One part of the legislative history, which we pointed out to the court, was the belief that teachers needed to learn about the coming year's students and that, by attending IEP meetings, they could learn about the unique needs of particular children.

Senator Robert Stafford of Vermont, who authored the integration language in the EHA, had told his colleagues:

> An additional benefit that will result from these conferences is one that is too often overlooked. Not only will the child be better served, and the parents better informed of the limitations their child has due to a particular handicap, but the teacher will learn from this experience as well. As we look more and more toward children with handicaps being educated with their "normal" peers, we must realize, and try to alleviate, the burden put upon the teacher who must cope with that child and all the others in the class as well. The teacher needs reinforcement and a better understanding of the child's abilities and disabilities. It is hoped that participation in these IEP conferences will have a positive effect on the attitude of the teacher toward the child, and an understanding of the child's problems in relating to his or her peers because of a handicapping condition.[2]

The school position, however, remained the same: that IEP meetings were for special education personnel only.

Third, we pointed out that socialization was a legitimate interest to consider at the IEP meeting. We quoted the language of another federal district court, which had ruled that "interaction and involvement with classmates is an important part of the modern educational curriculum."[3] One federal circuit court of appeals had also stated that "in some cases, a placement which may be considered better for academic reasons may not be appropriate because of the failure to provide for mainstreaming."[4]

If it was not possible to get Danny's needs for interaction with non-disabled students met inside a classroom, we argued, it was appropriate to seek socialization activities outside the classroom, during lunch and recess. The regulations implementing the EHA provided that meals and recess should be targets for integration.[5] Regulations in Section 504 of the Rehabilitation Act made the same provision, stating that "this requirement is especially important for children whose educational needs necessitate their being solely with other handicapped children during most of each day."[6]

Fourth, we reminded the court that Danny needed opportunities to interact with nondisabled students not just for socialization. He also needed to develop language and behavior by being around normally speaking and acting peers. In the early childhood class, which included only students with disabilities, most more severe than Danny's, there were no such models. How would the school district meet Danny's developmental needs in a segregated setting? Danny's educational needs clearly required him to have some interactions with nondisabled students.

Finally, we argued to the court that it was unfair to punish Danny because his prekindergarten teacher did not know how to teach him. The legislative history of the EHA affirmed that students with disabilities were being denied access to programs because of a lack of trained personnel. We argued that his regular education teacher in prekindergarten had declined to learn how to deal with him: that she was unwilling to attend the IEP meeting, to follow an IEP plan, to coordinate efforts with Danny's other teacher, to read about Danny's condition, or to attend a conference about children like Danny. The hearing officer had found that the prekindergarten teacher was devoting 100 percent of her time to dealing with Danny. How much of her time would it take, we wondered, if she were trained to deal with him? The Supreme Court had reminded us that schools were required to have a comprehensive system of personnel development by which they would "acquire and disseminate . . . promising educational practices."[7] Where was such a plan here? Didn't Danny have a right to a teacher who knew how to teach him?

The district court judge disagreed, affirming the hearing officer's opinion. Danny's parents decided to appeal to the Fifth Circuit Court of Appeals. We reasserted the arguments we had made throughout the case and waited for the decision.

The Fifth Circuit decision in the case, *Daniel R.R. v. State Board of Education*,[8] began with a recognition of the tension between two requirements of the EHA: that the program offered be restrictive enough to confer educational benefit but that it be delivered in the least restrictive environment.[9] The school must assure that a program for a child with a disability confers educational benefit. If the regular education environment does not assure adequate benefit, then program restrictions (including supplemental aids and services and curriculum modifications) must be considered, even to the point of removing the child from regular education to self-contained special education. But at the same time, the school must assure that the approach chosen is no more restrictive than necessary and that inter-action with nondisabled students will occur.

The Fifth Circuit then disagreed with the district court decision in two significant ways. The district court had found Danny not qualified for consideration for the regular class because he could not master the essential elements of the curriculum required of other students in that class. The Fifth Circuit disagreed, noting that, with the passage of the EHA, Congress "[drew] handicapped chil-dren into the regular education environment," intending to tolerate differences:

> Given the tolerance embodied in the EHA, we cannot predicate access to regular education on a child's ability to perform on par with nonhandicapped children. . . . If the child's individual needs make mainstreaming appro-priate, we cannot deny the child's access to regular edu-cation simply because his educational achievement lags behind that of his classmates.[10]

The second point of disagreement was that the district court deci-sion had focused only on academic benefit when it considered whether Danny could receive benefit in the regular educational en-vironment. The Fifth Circuit stated that the district court placed "too much emphasis" on that element, for academic benefits

> are not mainstreaming's only virtue. Rather mainstream-ing may have benefits in and of itself. For example, the language and behavior models available from nonhandi-capped children may be essential or helpful to the handi-capped child's development. In other words, although a handicapped child may not be able to absorb all of the regular education curriculum, he may benefit from non-academic experiences in the regular education environment.[11]

How, then, does one determine if a particular child should be mainstreamed? The Fifth Circuit created a two-part inquiry. First, "we ask whether education in the regular classroom, with the use of supplemental aids and services, can be achieved satisfactorily for a given child."[12] To determine that, there are four subquestions:

1. "At the outset we must examine whether the state has taken steps to accommodate the handicapped child in regular education. The Act requires states to provide supplementary aids and services and to modify the regular education program when they mainstream handicapped children."[13] Our basic point had been won. Special education students do have a right to be in regular environments, to have modifications made in those environments, and to have supplementary aids and services in those environments to make the integrated program work.

   The Fifth Circuit went even further: "The Act does not permit states to make mere token gestures to accommodate handicapped students; its requirement for modifying and supplementing regular education is broad."[14] We were sure that the "mere token gestures" referred to were the crayons and scissors mentioned by the school district as its attempts at modification. Finally, on this point, the Fifth Circuit reminded us that this requirement, like many in the EHA, must be within reason. If the needed modifications would change the curriculum "beyond recognition" or result in the child's not being taught any of the skills normally taught in that class, then that would exceed the requirement.[15]

2. Once the court is assured that modifications will be available, "we examine whether the child will receive an educational benefit from regular education." This calls for balancing the nature and severity of the child's condition against the curriculum and goals of the regular class. The Fifth Circuit reminded us again that

   > academic achievement is not the only purpose of mainstreaming. Integrating a handicapped child into a nonhandicapped environment may be beneficial in and of itself. . . . For example, a child may be able to absorb only a minimal amount of the regular education program, but may benefit enormously from the language models that his nonhandicapped peers provide for him. In such a case, the benefit that the child receives from mainstreaming may tip the balance in favor of mainstreaming even if the child cannot flourish academically.[16]

More of our points had been won: When an integrated setting is considered, benefits other than academic ones are important. The parents did not have the wrong priorities, as the hearing officer had written; they were right in seeking language and behavior models for Danny in a regular education setting, even though he would not immediately obtain academic benefit.

3. Next, the court said, we should consider whether any detriment to the child will result from the proposed mainstreaming: "Indeed, mainstreaming a child who will suffer from the experience would violate the Act's mandate for a free appropriate public education."[17]

4. "Finally, we ask what effect the handicapped child's presence has on the regular classroom environment and, thus, on the education that the other students are receiving." The court noted that a mainstreamed child might engage in disruptive behavior, impairing the education of others, and that the EHA's regulations recognized that as inappropriate. Further, the child might require a great deal of the teacher's attention. The Fifth Circuit acknowledged that the EHA required schools to provide supplementary aids and services and thus contemplated that "a teaching assistant or an aide" might have to be considered. "If, however, the handicapped child requires so much of the teacher or the aide's time that the rest of the class suffers, then the balance will tip" in favor of removing the child from the regular education setting.[18]

Having established this test, the court then applied it to the facts of Danny's case as stated by the hearing officer after the hearing that had occurred 2 years previously. The court found that the state had made modifications possible through its regulations, that Danny had received very little academic benefit in his short exposure to the prekindergarten class but would benefit from the language and behavior models there, that there was evidence of detriment to Danny in the hearing officer's findings that the child had begun to stutter and that he sometimes covered his ears and climbed under his desk, and that Danny took enough of the teacher's and aide's time that it affected the education of the other students. Balancing those factors, the court decided that the proposed regular education prekindergarten class in September of 1986 was not appropriate for Danny.

The court then announced that, if a decision was made to remove a child from the regular education environment for a portion of a day, a second inquiry must occur:

We next ask whether the child has been mainstreamed to the maximum extent appropriate. The EHA and its regulations do not contemplate an all-or-nothing educational system in which handicapped children attend either regular or special education. Rather, the Act and its regulations require schools to offer a continuum of services. Thus, the school must take intermediate steps where appropriate, such as placing the child in regular education for some academic classes and in special education for others, mainstreaming the child for nonacademic classes only, or providing interaction with nonhandicapped children during lunch and recess.[19]

Applying this standard to Danny, the Fifth Circuit Court found that, in the fall of 1986, the school district was proposing enough mainstreaming by offering lunch and recess in integrated settings. It therefore affirmed the decision of the district court.

Danny's parents were shocked. They had lost. Or had they? The Fifth Circuit had adopted everything we had argued for. All of regular education was to be open to consideration for integration. The Fifth Circuit had specified that, if Danny were to need a self-contained class for one academic setting, all other settings were still to be considered for integration. The court had listed art, music, physical education, lunch, and recess as well as the academic classes.[20] The court had added its "hope" that the amount of integration would vary "as the child develops."[21]

By the time the decision was made, Danny was 2 years older and had developed far beyond the hearing officer's pessimistic prognosis. Danny's parents approached the public school and asked for a new IEP plan for the 1989–1990 school year, one based on the requirements of the *Daniel R. R.* opinion. The school began with a new evaluation and then held the IEP meeting at Danny's home school. (Prior IEP meetings, in contrast, had been held at the campus where the school had decided in advance to serve Danny.)

The IEP plan specified self-contained classes with other special education students for core academics. However, Danny was to have regular physical education and art. He would also be with other students for lunch and recess. Danny is now at his home school, so he has neighborhood friends. He has also made friends with nondisabled students in physical education and art, so he knows lots of children to eat with at lunch and play with at recess.

Danny now begins his day on the playground with other students, waiting for the class bell rather than reporting directly to a segregated class. On one recent day when his mother passed the playground on her way to meet with a teacher, Danny was talking to some non-disabled friends and swinging his book bag around. He saw his mother and called out to her, "I really like it out here." So do we, Danny.

# Notes

1. Board of Education v. Rowley, 458 U.S. 176 (1982), at 191.
2. Congressional Record, S10961, June 18, 1975.
3. Espino v. Besteiro, 520 F.Supp. 905 (S.D. TX 1981).
4. Roncker v. Walter, 700 F.2d 1058 (6th Cir. 1983)
5. 34 C.F.R. 300.553.
6. 34 C.F.R. 104.34(b). See also 34 C.F.R. 104–Appendix, paragraph 24.
7. Rowley, note 1, at 207.
8. Daniel R. R. v. State Board of Education, 874 F.2d 1036 (5th Cir. 1989).
9. Daniel R. R., at 1044.
10. Daniel R. R., at 1047.
11. Daniel R. R., at 1047–1048.
12. Daniel R. R., at 1048.
13. Daniel R. R., at 1048.
14. Daniel R. R., at 1048.
15. Daniel R. R., at 1048–1049.
16. Daniel R. R., at 1049.
17. Daniel R. R., at 1049.
18. Daniel R. R., at 1049–1050.
19. Daniel R. R., at 1050.
20. Daniel R. R., at 1050.
21. Daniel R. R., at 1050.

# Extended School Year

The *Rowley* decision established the requirement that school programs confer benefit. Some parents began to question whether their children were receiving benefit if what they had accomplished during the 9-month school year was lost during summer vacation. Similarly, some parents wondered if their children were receiving their due benefit during the school year if the programming called for in the IEP plan could not begin in September because months were needed to get the student back on track after a 3-month break in programming.

What really concerned Congress and the courts was whether youngsters with disabilities would be able to progress, during their educational experience, to a point of independence. Congress clearly wanted these young people to be able to live independently, if possible; to work independently, if possible; to move around in their communities, if possible; and to live a normal life span, if possible. The earliest cases to examine the question of extended school year services reflected the reality that, without appropriate programming, some youngsters would remain dependent in every aspect of their lives and in fact would have shortened life expectancies.[1]

Congress had, in the Education for All Handicapped Children Act amendments, extended the age range for services beyond the traditional 12-year school program. The legislators recognized that it took longer for some children to develop needed skills and that 12 years might not be enough. It was inconceivable, then, to imagine that a school would throw away 3 months of each year (the summer break in programming) if it meant that the student in question would lose ground each summer and conclude the school experience without quite attaining that threshold of independence. It was quite consistent with Congress's expressed intent that programming continue during the summer if that was required to prevent a deterioration of skills that would disrupt overall programming.

In the earliest cases to reach the courts, there was a simple legal principle. The school districts concerned had a firm policy banning any services beyond a 180-day school year. Those early cases were quickly won because such a ban obviously violated the requirements of the Education of the Handicapped Act (EHA) that decisions be based on individual needs and not on rigid policies.

The real issue now facing the courts was what criteria should be applied if a school had agreed to provide summer programming for any child who needed it but had determined that a particular child did not need such programming in order to benefit. Steven was the perfect student to raise that issue in what would become the leading case in the country on extended school year services.

Steven, as the court described him, suffers from cerebral dysplasia or hyperplasia, an abnormal development of the brain. His hands and face are affected. He has an unusual laxity in his joints, an uncoordinated gaze, and a significant lack of muscle tone. He can walk only with assistance. He has been diagnosed as severely mentally retarded, has frequent tantrums, and cannot communicate by oral expression, although he does communicate by pointing to pictures and symbols on a communication board.[2] The first time I met Steven he was watching a favorite TV show. He quickly pointed on his communication board to "Hello," paused a socially acceptable second, pointed to "Good-bye," and looked back at the TV.

Steven had been in a Head Start program, which had 12-month programming, and he had experienced progress until age 5. That summer there was a break in Steven's programming, followed by what the court called a limited education over the next 9-month school year,[3] followed by another summer break. By age 7 Steven had experienced a significant loss of the skills that he had gained in the Head Start program.

When Steven's mother moved into the present school district, her son was placed in a class for students with multiple disabilities. In the spring, the mother inquired about summer services because of the obvious setbacks Steven had suffered in the absence of programming during the previous three summers. She was told that the school district would offer only a month-long, half-day program, with no provision for transportation. According to school officials, that program decision was based not on Steven's needs but on cost[4] and on the fact that "Steven's teacher had declined to work that summer."[5] School officials also noted that they had offered an open enrollment program during the previous summers and had perceived a general lack of interest on the part of parents.

The record does not show clearly why Steven's mother did not elect to try the limited programming available during that summer. As a single parent, Steven's mother was obligated to arrange for his care during full days throughout the summer, and the court noted that perhaps "the lack of transportation and the hours made it impossible for Steven to attend."[6] In the absence of skilled programming over that summer, Steven's behavior deteriorated, and he regressed in his ability to stand, point, and feed himself.

During the next 9-month school year, Steven's mother began pressing for services for the following summer (the summer of 1981). Her requests, however, were flatly denied by the special education director, who stated that no summer services would be made available to Steven.[7] The mother's requests for summer services and transportation had never been submitted to an IEP committee; the decision apparently was made solely by the administrator. The mother appealed to a hearing officer, who issued an interim order requiring immediate convening of the IEP committee to consider the issue of summer services. That committee declined to provide services and offered only a request that a regional service center provide consultative services.

During the summer of 1981, when the school district was providing no services, Steven's mother located a child care center and educational program called the Learning Tree. The evidence showed that, by attending the Learning Tree during that summer, Steven advanced in his ability to communicate by means of his board and in his social and feeding skills. However, the evidence also suggested that, because Steven lacked structured physical training, he regressed in development of motor skills and mobility.[8] The court also noted that Steven's opportunity to interact with others during the summer, including other children, was beneficial in the development of his emotional behavior.[9]

The hearing was not concluded until the end of the summer of 1981. The hearing officer found that the school district should have provided summer services during the summer just past. He required the school to clarify its position and make a decision by March 1982 concerning the summer of that year.

The final order from the hearing officer required the school to provide full summer services for all succeeding summers, starting in 1982. The school district filed a complaint in federal court, appealing that order.

The school district held a meeting in the spring of 1982, as ordered, supposedly to plan summer programming. However, instead of discussing such programming, the district officials began to talk about placing Steven in an institution. School personnel focused on problems in controlling Steven's tantruming behavior. They insisted that the child's behavior posed a danger to himself and others and that he should be institutionalized. Under current state law, such a placement would mean that the local school district would have no further programming or fiscal responsibility regarding Steven.

Steven's mother had received no notice of the meeting content, as was required by law.[10] She had come prepared to discuss the justification for a summer program, but the school district had obviously come with a different—and rehearsed—agenda. Therefore, in direct violation of the hearing officer's order, the school officials never did discuss planning an extended school year program for Steven.

When it became apparent that school personnel would not discuss anything but institutionalization, Steven's mother left the meeting. The school district then voted in favor of placing Steven in an institution and filed an amended complaint in district court, claiming that, because the school district had now disposed of the matter, its duties had ended and the entire case should be dismissed. The district court rejected that argument.

For the summer of 1982, Steven's mother, once again left totally on her own, attempted to place Steven in some educational program in the community, but the court found that no programs were available.[11] The closest program that the mother could find was at the Warm Springs Rehabilitation Hospital, located so far from home that Steven had to reside there. At that facility he received diagnosis, evaluation, education, and training. He was given an educational program with a special education teacher and received physical, occupational, and speech therapy twice each day. While at Warm Springs, Steven developed the ability to walk approximately 30 feet between parallel bars, and he could walk perhaps 20 feet in a walker. He also made substantial progress in communication skills. This summer program cost Steven's mother $9776.[12]

The district court found that "the diagnosis, evaluation, education and training received by Steven at Warm Springs permitted him to avoid suffering severe and significant regression during June and July of 1982."[13] At the end of the summer, Steven required surgery on his hips and returned to school September 20. After a wheelchair accident he was out for another 2 weeks. The court found that, "as a result of the lack of a structured program between Steven's departure from Warm Springs and the healing period after his surgery, Steven regressed in his ability to walk."[14] Steven has not walked since that time.

As a result of a preliminary order by the district court in June 1983, the IEP committee met and agreed that Steven would be placed in a summer program, with the assistance of an aide and with related services "to the same or greater extent as provided during the regular school year."[15] It was further agreed that the school district would be responsible for the costs of transporting Steven to and from the program. In response to the preliminary and permanent injunctive relief granted by the district court, the school district has since provided Steven full summer programming, with a teacher, an aide, and consultative services.[16]

The district court reached its final decision in 1984. It found the school district's policies to have violated the EHA, Section 504 of the Rehabilitation Act, and the Equal Protection Clause of the Fourteenth Amendment of the United States Constitution. The court found that the school district had been basing programming decisions for children with disabilities on a predetermined policy rather than on the individual needs of the child. The court questioned "whether the [school district] values fiscal concerns over the needs of handicapped children."[17]

The court found that the school district had (even though the district denied this) a policy of providing no educational services over the summer because no special education student had been provided programming beyond the 180-day school term, nor were summer services ever recommended by an IEP committee.

The court applied the *Rowley* standard to Steven in a very simple way. *Rowley* requires answers to two questions: Were the procedures of the EHA complied with, and did the resulting IEP plan confer benefit? The court found that the first criterion was violated when the school district refused to give the child individual consideration as required by the EHA.[18] The second criterion—the conferring of benefit—was violated in two ways. Not only was the previous school year's benefit jeopardized by regression during the summer, the chance of benefit in the coming year was jeopardized as well: "Steven will not benefit from his educational program at the beginning of the 9-month academic year due to the necessary recoupment time for regression suffered over the summer months."[19]

The district court then explained the reason for the extended school year in a paragraph that has been accepted as the basic standard:

> Without some kind of continuous, structured educational program during the summer months, Steven will regress in skills learned and knowledge gained in the previous 180-day academic year. Although the Court has insufficient evidence to conclude that Steven would definitely suffer severe regression after a summer without such a program, neither can it conclude that he would not and there is evidence that shows that Steven has suffered more than the loss of skills in isolated instances and that he has required recoupment time of more than several

weeks after summers without continuous, structured programming. A summer without continuous structured programming would result in substantial regression of knowledge gained and skills learned, and, given the severity of Steven's handicaps, this regression would be significant.[20]

The district court concluded by saying, "The Court would make clear that the [school district] must provide some form of continuous, structured summer placement whether it believes that Steven would suffer severe regression without such placement or not."[21] The court noted that the school district did not have teachers on contract over the summer and that it might not qualify for state education agency reimbursement for summer services. Nevertheless, the court said, the school district was required to provide a program even if it had to do so by contracting through private sources.[22]

The school district continued to provide summer services but appealed the district court opinion to the Fifth Circuit Court of Appeals. I was granted permission by the Fifth Circuit to enter the case as an amicus curiae on several issues.

The attorneys representing Steven were doing a wonderful job and would clearly win the case at the Fifth Circuit, but my involvement had been requested by representatives of other children who would be directly affected by this decision. This could become the first case in the country to lay down a standard that would enable parents to tell whether they had a reason to argue for summer services for their child and that, conversely, would help schools to determine policies in setting up summer programs.

I reminded the Fifth Circuit that it had ruled the previous year in regard to an extended school year case. The court had, in that decision, *Crawford v. Pittman*,[23] emphasized how individualized decision making at the IEP meeting was central to the intent of the EHA:

> The Act requires the State to treat each child as an individual, a human whose unique qualities and needs can be evaluated and served only by a plan designed with wisdom, care and educational expertise. Its grand design does not tolerate policies that impose a rigid pattern on the education of children.[24]

The school district had, in fact, offered *something* in the way of summer services during one of the summers in contention; it had offered a month-long, half-day program. Steven's mother had decided not to enroll her son in that program. Would Steven have received some benefit had he attended that minimal program? We did not have to contend with that issue because the first criterion of the *Rowley* test asked whether the Act's procedures had been complied with. Those procedures require individualized decision making and no pre-determined policies. We reminded the Fifth Circuit that, in *Crawford*, it had also said, "Categorical limitations on the possible duration of special education programs are simply inconsistent with the Act's insistence on IEPs formulated to meet the unique needs of each handicapped child."[25]

The school district had not complied with the required procedures: It had a policy that denied individual decision making concerning extended school year services; it did not provide adequate notice to the parent before an IEP meeting at which extended school year services were to be discussed; and it refused to consider extended school year services at that meeting. At one juncture, no meeting was even convened, and the decision to deny extended school year services was simply made by the special education director. The Act's procedures had clearly not been complied with.

But the second criterion of the *Rowley* test dealt with benefit. The benefit did not have to maximize the student's potential, so a legitimate question was whether Steven would receive a legally adequate level of benefit in some minimal program and was, therefore, not entitled to a fuller program that would offer more benefit.

How could the court formulate a standard somewhere between regression so severe that it would negate the benefit that was otherwise legally sufficient for the previous 9-month school year and benefit so great that it would seem to approach maximization? The Fifth Circuit approached it in this way:

> As we stated in *Crawford v. Pittman*, the basic substantive standard under the Act, then, is that each IEP must be formulated to provide some educational benefit to the child, in accordance with the unique needs of that child. The some educational benefit standard does not mean that the requirements of the Act are satisfied as long as the handicapped child's progress, absent summer services, is not brought to a virtual standstill. Rather, if a child would experience severe or substantial regression during the summer months in the absence of a summer program, the handicapped child may be entitled to year round services. The issue is whether the benefits accrued to the child during the regular school year will be significantly jeopardized if he is not provided an educational program during the summer months.[26]

In the first case concerning extended school year to reach the circuit court level, *Battle v. Pennsylvania*,[27] the court argued about the benefit standard. How much regression over the summer months was necessary to support the argument that no benefit had been conferred during the previous 9 months? Would all the gains of the previous 9 months have to be canceled out and progress brought to a "virtual standstill"? Would the loss have to be even more extreme, with the absence of summer programming actually causing the child to lose ground by comparison with the start of the previous year? The Fifth Circuit adopted the concurring opinion in *Battle*,[28] which said that the absence of programming need not completely negate the gains of the previous school year but simply place them in jeopardy.

This opinion underscored another important point. The decision about extended school year programming would be made prospectively. That is, does a look at next summer suggest that the absence of continuous, structured programming will result in substantial jeopardy to this year's gains? Many school districts have attempted to answer that question retrospectively by looking at the absence of programming in the previous summer and seeing how much regression actually occurred. In this case, however, Steven had been receiving educational services for the four summers preceding the Fifth Circuit decision. In 1982 he had attended the private Warm Springs program, and since the court order of 1983 he had received school district-supplied programming during the summers. As a consequence he had not regressed, so any attempt to base a decision on regression would fail.

The district court had ordered, "Finally, the Court would make clear that the [school district] must provide some form of continuous, structured placement whether it believes Steven would suffer severe regression without such placement or not."[29] Further, the court noted that "although the Court had insufficient evidence to conclude that Steven would definitely suffer severe regression after a summer without such programming, neither can it conclude he would not."[30] Thus, the courts were saying that the decision about summer programming was an individualized one and that "given the severity of Steven's handicaps, this regression would be significant." Even though Steven had not regressed over the past several summers, his disabilities were still the same, and, given the severity of those disabilities, it was easy to see that his skill levels are always in jeopardy and any degree of regression would be significant.

Some commentators have differentiated between skills that can be learned and maintained over a period of time, then developed further, and other "emerging" skills that must continually be stimulated or be lost. For Steven, such an emerging skill was obviously the ability to walk. The court was quite struck with the fact that Steven was, at one point, on the brink of self-ambulation and the independence that skill implied. As the court noted, Steven lost that emerging skill through the absence of programming and the lack of competent staff. That skill, once gone, never returned. Thus, the prospective decision —whether the absence of programming in the upcoming summer will jeopardize developing skills—means that all of the skills being developed in the child must be considered and any skill that might be in jeopardy must be addressed in programming.

The decision reached in Steven's case does not mean that any degree of possible regression in the absence of programming is an automatic indication for continued programming. The child might regress in a way that is not significant, or the child might catch up quickly in the fall and be back on track. What this decision requires is that schools attend to children whose specific disabilities make them vulnerable to severe deterioration in skills that they have attained. This may be the case either because skill deterioration over the summer will place the previous year's benefit in question or because that deterioration will hamper the start of the following year's programming and thus undercut the benefit anticipated in the IEP.

It is also clear in this decision that what is being addressed are not just cognitive skills or academic achievements but the full range of a child's needs. A child who is not in jeopardy academically but who has, for example, physical or communication needs might receive summer programming that meets those needs.

The final issue that was addressed in Steven's case is what happens when the parent is not willing to sit still for a school district's unilateral decision that no services will be provided over the summer and goes out and privately procures services? What is the standard for reimbursement? Can the parent get back whatever is paid out?

This case not only stands currently as the leading decision on extended school year services in the United States, but it also has established the standard for parental reimbursement for privately procured services. That story is told in chapter 11.

# Notes

1. Battle v. Pennsylvania, 629 F.2d 269 (3rd Cir. 1980).
2. Alamo Heights v. State Board of Education, 790 F.2d 1153 (5th Cir. 1986), at 1155. Hereinafter I will distinguish this circuit court decision from the district court decision by referring to it as Circuit Court.

3. Alamo Heights Independent School District v. Williams, unpublished opinion (W.D. TX May 25, 1984), at 8. This decision will be referred to as District Court.
4. Circuit Court, at 1156.
5. District Court, at 8.
6. Circuit Court, at 1156.
7. District Court, at 8–9.
8. Circuit Court, at 1156–1157.
9. District Court, at 12.
10. 34 C.F.R. 300.504, 505.
11. District Court, at 13.
12. Circuit Court, at 1157; District Court, at 13.
13. District Court, at 14.
14. District Court, at 14.
15. District Court, at 14.
16. Circuit Court, at 1157.
17. District Court, at 29.
18. District Court, at 22 and 33.
19. District Court, at 33.
20. Circuit Court, at 1157.
21. District Court, at 33.
22. District Court, at 33–34.
23. Crawford v. Pittman, 708 F.2d 1028 (5th Cir. 1983).
24. Crawford, at 1030.
25. Crawford, at 1034.
26. Circuit Court, at 1158.
27. Note 1, supra.
28. Battle, at 282.
29. District Court, at 21.
30. District Court, at 15.

# Extended School Day

I began my brief to the United States Supreme Court by saying, "This case involves a parent driven to seek private services at private expense to supplement a rigid and inadequate public school program for her child."

The previous chapter dealt with a situation in which the school's rigid policy against extending school services into the summer months kept the student from achieving an appropriate education. But what if a student could not receive an appropriate education within the traditional 6-hour school day? Would a rigid rule prohibiting extension of services into the evening hours also be illegal?

By the time I began representing Sterling, two circuit courts of appeals had spoken on the issue. The Third Circuit had ruled in a case, *Kruelle v. New Castle County School District*,[1] where the school had refused to program for more than 6 hours per day. That court had also given us the first summer school case, and it emphasized the similarity in the two arguments:

> The trial judge's conclusion that Paul required more con-
> tinuous care is supported generally by the logic of the
> decision in *Battle v. Commonwealth of Pennsylvania* [the
> summer school case] and more specifically by analogous
> case law emerging in other federal courts. Just as in
> *Battle* we held that the *per se* application of the 180
> school-day rule accepted as appropriate for the nonhandi-
> capped cannot be presumed to satisfy the unique needs
> of handicapped children, here the school authorities are
> incorrect to assume that conforming to the six-hour day
> that suffices for nonhandicapped children will similarly
> fulfill their obligations with respect to Paul.[2]

The Fifth Circuit Court of Appeals had also ruled in regard to the summer school issue, in *Crawford v. Pittman*,[3] with language that seemed applicable to extended school days. The Fifth Circuit had described the Education of the Handicapped Act (EHA) by stating, "Its grand design does not tolerate policies that impose a rigid pattern on the education of children."[4] The Fifth Circuit then went on to say in *Crawford* that the Supreme Court's *Rowley* decision supported the *Kruelle* decision:

> The Supreme Court's decision in *Rowley* also recognized the Act's emphasis on individual consideration. The decision, therefore, implicitly ratifies the Third Circuit's conclusion that categorical limitations on the possible duration of special education programs are simply inconsistent with the Act's insistence on IEPs formulated to meet the unique needs of each handicapped child.[5]

But that is what had happened to Sterling, a youngster severely disabled by infantile autism. The categorical limitation of a 6-hour school day had rendered his education worthless. Worse, it was harming him.

The hearing officer's decision in Sterling's case described the youngster's disabilities and the history leading up to this litigation, noting that Sterling's autism resulted in a severe inability to generalize learning, a severe inability to communicate, and severe self-stimulating, self-abusive, aggressive, disruptive, and bizarre behavior.[6]

Sterling's mother, a single parent, began searching for special services for him before he was a year old. The family then lived in Louisiana, and the mother located a speech and hearing clinic at the University of Southern Mississippi. After a period of driving 100 miles each day, Sterling's mother moved to the town in which the clinic was located. When Sterling was 3, they moved again to enroll him in a private school.

When Sterling was almost 5, the family moved again, to my state, to enroll the youngster in a program called the Autistic Treatment Center. Sterling attended the program as a day student, at his mother's expense. In the 8 months he was there he made substantial progress. When Sterling became eligible for services from the public school in January of that year, the public school enrolled him in a co-op program. During the remaining 5 months of that school year, Sterling's speech, behavior, and self-help skills began to deteriorate.

During July and August, the public school offered no services whatsoever. By September, Sterling's problems had become so unmanageable that his mother withdrew him from the public school program and placed him again as a day student at the Autistic Treatment Center. The day program was not enough, and by November Sterling was a full-time residential student with an extended-day program that continued for the next 6 months. During that time Sterling's mother frequently observed and participated in his program and took him home for overnight stays. During the 6 months in the residential program Sterling progressed significantly in speech, behavior, and self-help skills.

For financial reasons, Sterling's mother changed her son's status to that of day student for the next 4 months, and in August she reenrolled him in the public school program. Once again he regressed. After 5 months in the public school, Sterling was uncontrollable. His behavior had become injurious to himself and others. By February a psychiatrist was urging Sterling's mother to place him in the Children's Medical Center, where he remained for 7 weeks.

Having become stabilized in the hospital, Sterling returned to the public school program in April and began to worsen. As in the previous year the public school offered nothing in July and August, so Sterling's mother took her son to a special clinic for a 5-day evaluation. Given the results of the evaluation and the child's further deterioration in July and August, the mother asked the school district for programming that would last more than just 6 hours per day and 9½ months per year.

The school district held an IEP meeting to discuss this request and again refused. The school personnel, reviewing all the information, insisted that Sterling was doing all right and could receive everything he needed in 6 hours per day of programming. The school district representative who headed the IEP committee later gave us an affidavit stating that she knew at the time that Sterling was regressing in her program and that he needed more. However, she felt constrained to ignore her professional opinion and act solely as an employee of the school district. Knowing that the school district wanted no student to have more than 6 hours per day of programming, she wrote on the IEP plan that 6 hours would meet Sterling's needs.[7]

Sterling's mother asked for an administrative hearing. A psychiatrist widely known as an expert on autism testified at the hearing that "Sterling is probably one of the three or four worst I've seen and the youngest—he's the worst I've seen at his age."[8] The hearing officer found that Sterling had needs in three areas—generalization of learning, communication skills, and control of severely self-abusive and aggressive behaviors—and that the public school program did not address them.[9]

The problem of generalization was not even addressed in the public school IEP plan. The need for communication skills was addressed, but the relevant programming was to be carried out only 2 hours per week. The speech therapist assigned to Sterling testified that she did not understand what the program should entail. The expert witness testified that Sterling needed training in communication skills the entire time he was being worked with.

The worst failure was in the area of self-injurious and aggressive behavior. It is clear that the public school program did not help Sterling; it is hard to tell whether it actually aggravated his problem. The record from the hearing showed that the public school personnel were forced to resort to using restraints (such as a helmet, a harness, and gauze hand wraps) and tying Sterling into a chair. Sterling had become uncontrollable on the school bus and, while riding the bus, was bound by his hands, ankles, and waist to the bus seat. When Sterling became aggressive at school, the teacher would simply call his mother and tell her to come and pick him up. Sterling's mother observed one incident in the classroom when the teacher, unable to control the boy, instructed an older student to catch Sterling and hold his head between the older student's knees.[10]

One very clear example of regression occurred while Sterling was in the public school program. While at the Autistic Treatment Center, Sterling had been able to sit in a regular classroom chair, voluntarily and without restraints. In the public school, however, he regressed to the point that he was placed in a lapboard chair. A goal stated in Sterling's IEP plan was for Sterling to move to a retainer chair with only a waist strap and then to a regular chair. He never attained this goal in the public school program. When Sterling was placed again at the Autistic Treatment Center he was able to achieve that goal. However, when he returned to the public school program, he regressed to the point that he was again in a lapboard chair.

The hearing officer found that Sterling could not receive an appropriate education in a 6-hour-a-day program run by the public school. If Sterling were to stay in the public school program, the hearing officer found, his future would be "a life of physical restraints and increasing medication, and eventually, no doubt, a state institution."[11] On the other hand, the experts' prognosis was that, with an appropriate program, "Sterling [would] attain the degree of independence required to live in a sheltered environment with community contact, and work in a sheltered workshop."[12]

The hearing officer also found "that Sterling's mother has, at all times, fully extended her time, efforts and financial resources to provide her son the special education he so urgently needs. Her conduct demonstrates a strong preference to keep Sterling at home and in a day program."[13]

The hearing officer ordered that the public school make available, at public expense, a residential placement for Sterling. His mother preferred a program that would allow Sterling to live at home but would extend his school day beyond 6 hours per day and extend his school week beyond 5 days.

The school district vigorously disagreed and appealed the hearing officer's opinion into court. The district also asked the court to terminate Sterling's mother's parental rights and make Sterling a ward of the state. If that were done, the school district would not have to pay a penny for Sterling's programming, and Sterling would be placed in a state institution. The school district officials contended that Sterling's mother was guilty of child neglect. They claimed that their duties ended and her parental duties began when the school bell rang. Thus, if she wanted the school to offer more than a 6-hour day, she was asking the state to assume her parental duties.

When depositions were taken of school personnel, the superintendent was asked whether, if Sterling's mother had placed her child in a private facility and paid for it herself, she would be a neglectful parent. The answer was no. (Only if Sterling's mother cost the school district money, it seemed, would they consider her neglectful.)

We were able to use that patently unfair attack on Sterling's mother to our advantage, confronting the school district with it at each level of court. For school district officials to win, they needed to be able to allege that they were willing to consider extended-day programming, that they could provide it, and that they rejected it only because Sterling did not need it. However, their action in court placed them in a logical bind: Their argument that anything beyond a 6-hour day equaled parental neglect meant that they could never claim willingness to consider anything more than a 6-hour day.

While the case was being appealed, the public school refused to make any changes in Sterling's program. After 3 months, his mother decided to supplement his program at her own expense. One staff person at the Autistic Treatment Center had been "highly successful" with Sterling and had not relied on restraints.[14] Sterling's mother hired him in May to work in her home, after school hours and on weekends, to extend Sterling's school day and school week.

At the end of the school year, this consultant accompanied Sterling's mother to a meeting with public school personnel. The public school hired the consultant to work with Sterling in its day program. For the rest of that school year, he worked in the public school day program and then worked for Sterling's mother after school and on weekends. During the summer, when the public school offered nothing, the consultant worked full time. That arrangement (school day as a public school consultant and evenings as a private consultant) continued into the next school year, until the consultant moved to another town to take a full-time job as director of a center for autistic children.

A few months later, Sterling's family moved to another school district. The public school immediately moved to have the lawsuit dismissed as moot, and the federal district court dismissed the case. We appealed to the circuit court of appeals on the grounds that the claim was not moot: Sterling's mother was owed reimbursement for private expenses incurred in supplementing the inadequate public school program.

In opposing that claim, the public school argued that the family's expenses had been for child care, referring to her consultant as a babysitter. Before 3:00 P.M. he was the school district's expert working with Sterling at school, and after 3:00 P.M., when he continued the same strategies with the youngster, he was a babysitter.

The Fifth Circuit agreed with our position and sent the case back to the district court for a full hearing. The public school appealed the circuit court decision, asking the United States Supreme Court to review it. We opposed the Supreme Court's taking the case and filed our brief.

We reminded the Supreme Court of the standard it had set in *Rowley:* whether the IEP plan is reasonably calculated to enable the child to receive educational benefits. We said that the public school standard, by contrast, was whether the IEP plan is reasonably calculated to fit within their budget. We told the Court about the school district employee's affidavit stating that the IEP plan was predetermined, that she did not exercise independent professional judgment but rather echoed the district's position. We told the Court how the public school had attacked Sterling's mother and asked that her parental rights be terminated.

We said that we wanted the case to be sent back to district court so that we could develop a full factual record. We asked in our respondents' brief in opposition to writ of certiorari for an opportunity to demonstrate the school officials' "hopelessly inadequate programming; their callous disregard for the education and well-being of a child; their intentional procedural violations that deny any parental input and make a hoax out of the IEP process; and their policy of seeking to terminate the parental rights of a parent who challenges them." The Supreme Court agreed with our position and sent us back to the district court. That court's ruling gave us exactly what we had hoped for on the issue of extended-day services:

> It is the conclusion of this court that the IEP developed
> by the school district was not reasonably calculated to

enable the child to receive educational benefit. The record is replete with evidence that Sterling made little or no forward progress under the IEP developed by the school district, and in fact, his condition deteriorated when he was removed from residential placement situations and placed in the [public school] program. . . . In this case, a proper IEP would have provided for extensive training and monitoring of Sterling on a twenty-four hour per day basis. That was the conclusion of the impartial hearing officer, and that is the conclusion adopted by this Court. [Sterling's mother], in obtaining additional help beyond that provided by the school district under the IEP, recognized that Sterling needed a more comprehensive program. That the services she obtained were not precisely what was ultimately determined appropriate is of no consequence in this case. The record supports the conclusion that [Sterling's mother] could not afford continuous residential placement. The services she obtained were intended by her to accomplish, within the bounds imposed by her financial situation, as close a facsimile of residential placement as possible. She should not, at this juncture, be faced with an empty victory because she possessed insufficient means to give her son the education she sought for him from the school district.[15]

With that decision, the school district's resolve seemed to disappear. We reached a settlement in which Sterling's mother received every penny she had paid for private services and we obtained our attorneys' fees. We had established the right of a student to have his needs considered for extended-day programming and the right of a parent to privately procure extended-day services and be reimbursed for expenses that a proper IEP plan would have provided.

## Notes

1. Kruelle v. New Castle County School District, 642 F.2d 687 (3rd Cir. 1981).
2. Kruelle, at 693.
3. Crawford v. Pittman, 708 F.2d 1028 (5th Cir. 1983).
4. Crawford, at 1030.
5. Crawford, at 1034.
6. In re: Garland Independent School District, EHLR 503:265 (1982).

7. Garland Independent School District v. Wilks, 657 F.Supp. 1163 (N.D. TX 1987).
8. In re: Garland, note 6, supra, at 268.
9. In re: Garland, at 268–272.
10. In re: Garland, at 266–267.
11. In re: Garland, at 272.
12. In re: Garland, at 272.
13. In re: Garland, at 272.
14. In re: Garland, at 270.
15. Wilks, note 7, supra, at 1166–1167.

# State Education Agency Responsibility

At the time the Education of the Handicapped Act (EHA) was passed, *Gary W. v. State of Louisiana*[1] was being played out in the courts and in the newspapers. That case involved the placement of children by Louisiana agencies into a variety of facilities in other states where standards were very low. An expert witness for the plaintiffs described one facility in my state as a place for children to die.

I couldn't believe or accept the attitude of private or public officials that there was no hope for these children because if there were not, why should anyone bother to program for them? With that attitude prevailing, hopelessness would become a self-fulfilling prophecy.

I confronted such a situation in a public program in what were known in our state as "schools for the retarded" with a young African-American man who had retardation and needed kidney dialysis. The public agency denied the request for dialysis. The attitude, we discovered, was "Why bother?" because it was expected that, however long the young man lived, he would just die in a state school anyway. A lawsuit was able to force dialysis, and the young man was eventually placed in a group home in the community, where he received a transplant and lives today.

That attitude of stereotyping, of gross generalization about an inevitable dead end for state school residents, seemed pervasive. I had helped draft a statute, adopted overwhelmingly by our state legislature, that removed stereotyping and stigmatizing language from 198 state statutes that had included terms such as *idiot, imbecile, moron,*

---

Jimmy is an assumed name representing the more than 1,700 youngsters who were state school residents in a class action suit, Griffith v. Bynum, Civ. No. A–82–CA–195 (W.D. TX 1985).

81

*crippled,* and *lunatic.* (Maybe a generation of staff and citizens who do not hear these words used so sweepingly will look at individuals rather than labels.) But I did not expect to encounter such negative stereotyping in the offices of our state education agency.

When the EHA was passed, Congress was worried about the large numbers of school-age youngsters in public institutions receiving no educational programming. Congress quite clearly required that the state education agency assume responsibility for all school-age children wherever they might be served (or unserved).[2] This population included youngsters in private schools and in all programs run by other state agencies, such as schools for citizens with retardation.

While other children in my state began to benefit from the implementation of the EHA, with its focus on individual evaluation and annual review of programming, the school-age residents of our state schools did not. The stereotype was that they were hopeless and that they functioned at a level below educability. Why else, we were asked, would they have been placed there by parents or other state agencies? They were going to live there the rest of their lives, weren't they? So why bother?

An additional stereotype applied to some was that they were so medically fragile that nothing could be done for them. When I first confronted the state director of special education about the state agency's responsibility to ensure appropriate programming for these youngsters, she said that she had been told, "They're like doorknobs; you just turn them every now and then." We discovered that some of the children were near comatose, and, for them, repositioning did appear to be the extent of the programming. But the mental image held by the state agency official (who told me that she had never visited any of the facilities) was wrong for the vast majority of the over 1700 school-age children there. And even those functioning at the lowest levels had a right to programming—a right that will be discussed shortly.

Our litigation strategy was simple: We wanted to assure proper programming, based on individual needs, for all of these children. What we found, however, as we visited facilities to document the case, were programs aimed at containment of individuals who were perceived to be there because the outside world did not want them. They were therefore being shaped toward acceptable institutional behaviors, compliant behaviors that they would need to tolerate a lifetime in an institution and that made work easier for the staff who were warehousing them.

How could such young people be taught behaviors necessary to function in the outside world when they were housed in large group settings? These youngsters had never seen a public school, never ridden a bus, never crossed a street unaided, never gone through the lunch line in a school cafeteria, never had an opportunity for extra-curricular activities. And they had certainly never been exposed to nondisabled children. The "norm" in which they learned and ac-quired behavior was the large dayroom filled with youngsters exhibit-ing bizarre and unproductive behaviors.

Congress was wise enough in developing the EHA to recognize the antidote of exposure to the real world. If we place people with dis-abilities in contact with nondisabled people, the real norm by which we all must live, we get a sense of what we are programming for. We work to develop behaviors that will specifically enable children to interact more readily with nondisabled peers. We work to eliminate behaviors that will keep children apart. We target for development the ability to communicate, to live as independently as possible, to care for basic personal needs, to travel in the community, and even-tually to have some sort of job.

But the most important thing that needs development in anyone is the person's self-concept. How badly had these students' self-concepts been damaged? When everyone around a child says, "Why bother?" then why should the one who is the subject of so much negative programming bother? To what extent were the situations that we found in state schools merely self-fulfilling prophecies caused by inattention, neglect, and lack of educational resources? What would happen with these children if someone did start to bother?

Our experts in the litigation looked at evaluation reports and writ-ten plans for a cross section of youngsters. They found not the kinds of evaluations that are performed in public schools—evaluations that look for capabilities and explore possibilities—but rather evaluations that were all diagnosis and no prescription. The written plans (cer-tainly not IEP plans as required in the federal statute) were static, not dynamic. They recorded the child's annual decline rather than plan-ning annual growth and allocating sufficient resources so that the child could reasonably be expected to attain annual goals.

The state education agency continued to look the other way and deny any responsibility. It declined to monitor for program violations. We discovered that it in fact had recently monitored some of the state facilities, but we were never able to discover the subject of the monitoring. None of the 1,700 school-age youngsters in 12 state schools had been found not to be served in compliance with the federal statutes.

The official response to our lawsuit by the State Department of Mental Health and Mental Retardation was that they were in full com-pliance with all relevant statutes. The official response by the co-defendant state education agency, issued repeatedly by its general counsel and its state special education director, was that parents had placed their children in those facilities and had thereby waived their children's right to any claim under the federal statutes. Not only was that legally ridiculous, the reality was that most of those youngsters had been placed there by parents who were told they had no other choice. Others were there because local public schools said they could not serve the youngsters and steered them into what turned out to be lifelong institutionalization.

It was clear what our lawsuit had to do. First, it had to establish that the responsibility for these children belonged with the state education agency. Second, it had to bring the children into the light of day by exposing them to their peers in regular public schools. Third, it had to end the placement of school-age children in dead-end facilities like those state schools.

As the litigation heated up and we drafted a proposed order for the court, the opposition from both state agencies suddenly vanished. We had certainly generated publicity that was adverse to the state school system. We had brought the state education agency's noncompliance to the attention of federal funding authorities in Washington. We had contacted the Office for Civil Rights because Section 504 of the Rehabilitation Act clearly requires that persons in institutions have opportunities for interaction with nondisabled persons.[3] Something caused a dramatic change, and the state agencies agreed to a settlement of the litigation.

The implementation of our order required that the youngsters at state facilities be educated by the local public schools in whose geographical areas the state facilities were located. Some of those public schools were very large, and adding the state school students to their census was no problem. However, the state had a practice of placing its facilities in remote areas, and the result was that several large groups of youngsters would be attending small public schools. One local public school would have its census of special education students doubled.

There was immediate resistance. None of the 12 local public schools who would serve these students had been defendants to the lawsuit. They had not been sued because they had not done anything wrong. We had sued the state education agency and the state schools, and we had made clear in the settlement negotiations that the state assumption of responsibility would include a state assumption of funding so that there would be no economic burden on local districts. We began visiting all the local districts when we heard the rumor that they planned to sue to set aside the order.

As part of the order the state education agency was required to designate one individual to oversee the youngsters' concerns, and it hired the one person who I could imagine was capable of carrying off this transition. When we appeared together at local schools, talked to officials, and visited state facilities, he was an outspoken advocate for these children. It had been easy, through our lawsuit, to point out the problems, but actually solving the problems was much more difficult. This one individual was indispensable to the solution. I do not know what he said to the local districts when I was not with him, but it must have been very effective because the initial hostility and opposition melted away.

I had taken a conservative approach to implementation. I had insisted on a 3-year phase-in of these youngsters to local public schools and was attacked by some groups for selling out. Every child, on day one of the implementation order, would come under the full scrutiny of the EHA and begin receiving services from the local public schools. But not every child would actually attend a local public school on that first day. We were going to follow the orderly process of evaluation and IEP programming to determine appropriate placements. We were not simply going to dump these children in local public schools; that would guarantee failure and backlash.

The latter approach was exactly what one spokesperson for the state schools insisted on. Now that we had exposed the fact that these institutions were not "schools" and were not meeting the responsibilities outlined in the EHA, and we had arranged for others to accept responsibility for programming during the school day, that individual wanted the school-age youth out immediately. I accused him of wanting a guaranteed failure in the local public schools so that the state schools would look good by comparison.

The state schools had also provided what the EHA referred to as related services, such as physical therapy. Our state had been too stingy with funding to ensure related services adequate to the educational needs of any child, but at least the state schools had therapists. Now that local public schools were expected to provide related services, the state schools wanted to cancel the therapists. They no longer wanted to provide physical therapy: That was now the local schools' duty. The bitterest fight we faced during settlement negotiations was from the state school representative who, before settlement, had claimed that everything was fine within the state schools but who now became a neoadvocate insisting that every state school child must immediately go out to the local public schools and be fully served there.

I insisted that the first wave of youngsters to hit the local public schools be success stories. Although youngsters were being evaluated for the first time in compliance with the standards of the EHA, we were also evaluating the local schools. My colleague in implementation from the state education agency was looking at school capability and staffing. He retained several consultants who were able to go into the schools and put together programs that would meet the needs of particular children who were entering.

Congress had seen the need for such evaluation all across the country. At the time of passage of the EHA, an estimated 1 million students were being denied public education. Congress required a comprehensive system of personnel development that would identify needs and then upgrade school staff capabilities to meet those needs.[4] The idea is simple and indispensable to effective programming, but I had never seen it work the way Congress intended until now. (Unfortunately, I have not seen it work since.)

Most of the state school children had deficits in behavior that called for programming to develop speech, self-care skills, social interaction skills, or vocational skills. Others, however, had behavioral excesses that would be quite disruptive in a local public school. Those were top priority for programming.

Where we discovered youngsters with severe behavioral problems, we attempted to program for those behaviors before the school transition occurred. Because the local school personnel were providing education (at the local school as students integrated into that setting and on the state school campus for students who had not yet moved), they could learn techniques of behavior management and also help us assess when those students could constructively be integrated into the local environment. All the students were to be integrated at the end of 3 years, and the process actually moved more quickly than we expected.

For the students who remained on state school campuses during the school day, we now had a purpose for programming, an answer to the question "Why bother?" Their programs were targeted specifically toward the behaviors needed to achieve success in the public school environment. We wanted to give these youngsters a chance. We did not want to force them into a strange environment and then watch the local children withdraw from them. And we did not want them to be resegregated into self-contained classes so that all they got out of our effort was a bus ride.

The reaction at the local public schools was one of incredible relief. Their personnel had fallen heir to the stereotypes and assumptions that state school children were too different, too hopeless, too out of control for public school. Several administrators called me and exclaimed, "We are already serving kids in our district who are more disabled than the ones coming over from the state school!"

And then the administrators began sharing personal stories. Youngsters whose state school records had shown that they had never spoken or attempted to communicate, and who now, through assistive technology, had an opportunity to express themselves, were communicating.

One principal, on his first day at a new high school, decided to spend that day with the state school students. The state school had used an artificial approach of rewards and punishments, but these youngsters' behaviors now had to be shaped toward those that would be reinforced naturally in the general environment. The principal told me of working with a youngster on a short task. When the student completed the task successfully he looked the principal in the eye and said, "I did it. Now where's my damn Coke?"

There were some outcomes short of success. One high school accepted several youngsters who appeared ready to integrate fully into the life of the school. The first few periods of the day went well but then, in the free time after lunch, one student went to the front hall and systematically kicked out the glass in every one of the trophy cases. A behavior consultant addressed the structure that student would need to make a successful transition into less restrictive environments.

We found many school personnel puzzled because some of the students moving into their programs were functioning at a higher level than many other youngsters in special education. These new youngsters began to expose the unnecessary segregation that occurs in some public schools. In one such school, children with retardation all went to one facility and stayed there until age 22. Because our clients were backed by a court order requiring integration with nondisabled children to the maximum extent appropriate, we would not accept that kind of limit. We wanted our students to receive the special resources available in those self-contained programs, to the degree that they needed them, but we did not want the dead-end placements. We found some of our state school students with retardation leapfrogging over some comparable public school children into regular schools and vocational placements.

As the "easiest" youngsters moved into public school classes during the 3-year implementation, we began to see the children who were more difficult to program for, and many were medically fragile. We were warned that about 550 of the youngsters might die if moved from their present location. That seemed curious to us because, as we visited state schools, we saw many of those children boarded on carts and moved to a building that served as a day school, moved again for lunch, moved again to school, and then moved back to their residence.

We confronted one physician, who said that no one could leave the state school grounds without severe danger to his or her life. Further probing revealed the real problem: The physician's malpractice policy would not cover the youngsters off state school grounds. We felt that the public interest and the individual children's rights certainly outweighed the state schools' perception of increased liability.

We also knew that many of the medically fragile children had been victims of institutionalization. We wanted full evaluations to see whether these children were victims of their own disabilities or had been disabled by the environment in which they had been placed. The vast majority of the medically fragile children were eventually able to participate in the public school programs. Some children, tragically, seemed beyond the reach of any program. They appeared comatose. They did not seem to respond to any auditory stimulation. They did not track light with their eyes. Tactile stimulation seemed aversive— the children would curl away from anyone touching them.

Those children were still eligible for programming under the EHA, which establishes eligibility without regard to the nature or severity of the handicapping condition. However, the appropriate programs for those children, developed through evaluation and IEP con- ferences, were based on very basic stimulation and continual obser- vation to see if a program could be productively developed. Some of those children never seemed to respond. Some died. There were no miracles. No one "woke up" and boarded the bus for school as in some made-for-TV movie.

One of my most hopeless moments came when I was called aside to address a human rights committee. The youngster in question had never moved. Although a teenager, he had never rolled over or lifted himself up. He was repositioned constantly by staff but showed no response to any auditory, visual, or tactile stimulation. The boy had a swallow reflex and was fed very laboriously. He often choked and occasionally aspirated his food, requiring emergency procedures. To remedy this potentially life-threatening problem, the committee had recommended that a gastrostomy tube be inserted for feeding.

I was asked if that was a violation of his quality of life. The staff member framed the issue by saying that the only thing he could im- agine this youngster experiencing during the day was swallowing food and perhaps tasting it. If that experience were removed, the staff per- son asked, wouldn't that remove the only thing that made the boy's life worth living?

We talked a long time, and I was not empowered to answer that ques- tion. But I felt encouraged that a staff person was asking it. If we could worry about the quality of life of someone who functioned at a level that most of us could not even comprehend, then surely we would be concerned about the quality of life of youngsters who could attend public school daily and eventually disappear into our communities.

One small school district was so overwhelmed by the number of children who would be entering from the state school that the next school district up the road volunteered to take 12 youngsters. Before the start of the school year, school personnel built a ramp and made a school project of learning about the new students. The children made a huge welcome banner, which was draped across the building the first day the state school bus arrived. Students from the school newspaper interviewed the newcomers and told some of their stories.

From a legal standpoint those state school youngsters were not in the jurisdiction of the volunteer public school, and from a legal standpoint they were not that school's responsibility. But it wasn't a legal issue we were hoping to overcome—it was the human issue of realizing that these children belonged to all of us. That school's approach taught the best lesson of all.

My favorite individual stories came out of a rural area where the special education director absolutely embraced the youngsters. As his personnel saw these students during the school day and saw how much could be done for them, they began to wonder about the countereducational aspect of the youngsters' living in the state school at night. I had been used to arguing with public schools about clients' programs and being told, "We're doing a good job during the day, but it's that lousy home environment that is causing the problem." Now I was hearing a public school official say the same thing: "We can do wonders with these kids during the day, but they go back to that awful state school environment every night, and we have to start over again the next day."

The special education director pointed out the institutional shuffle that most of these children, required to walk in long lines, had developed. He had noticed that as these students walked freely on a local school campus, and saw their nondisabled peers walking, they lost the shuffle. The director had observed that the youngsters initially got off of the state school bus with their clothes in disarray, but after a few days in public school they began to take much more notice of their appearance. He told me of male students who would go to the restroom and return without having fully reclothed themselves. Peer pressure in the public school quickly corrected those behaviors.

This particular school had many after-school activities and weekend community programs. The special education director felt uncomfortable that some of his children went on to weekends rich with activity and others boarded a bus back to boredom. He began enlisting sponsors to "adopt" children and take them to community activities. Eventually the question kept arising: "Why are these children in a state school, anyway, because they can function so well in our community?" The director called me one day with the news that he had just received a substantial check from a local citizen. The donor wrote that, although he did not have a family member with a disability, he had seen what was being done with these children and wanted to help.

That seemed to me the only way to judge the success of this endeavor. When we shut these children away, whether in a state school physically removed from our lives or in a totally segregated program within a public school, they seem no longer our children or our responsibility. When we recognize that they are part of our community and part of our lives, then we find teachers who can program for them and citizens who can accept them. And we find the answer to the question "Why bother?"

# Notes

1. 437 F.Supp. 1209 (D. LA 1976).
2. 20 U.S.C. 1412(6). See also 34 C.F.R. 300.600(a)(2).
3. 34 C.F.R. 104.54.
4. 20 U.S.C. 1413(a)(3). See also 34 C.F.R. 300.380.

# Impartial Hearings

One of the major federal court decisions that launched the special education revolution was *Mills v. Board of Education*[1] in 1972. When Judge Waddy finished writing his decree in that case, he had a problem. He had just ordered sweeping changes in the way the public school had to conduct its business. Now he had to face the prospect that literally thousands of parents might claim that the school district was not properly implementing his decree. They might ask to come into court on contempt proceedings, clogging up the docket.

Judge Waddy's solution was to create a federal master, called an independent hearing officer,[2] to oversee implementation of the decree. Congress followed the model of the independent hearing officer when it created the Education of the Handicapped Act (EHA) 2 years later.

Although many schools assumed that a hearing officer would be an expert in special education, that person is not expected to be skilled in the subject matter being heard. A judge hearing a case is not supposed to reach a decision on the basis of previous knowledge and personal opinions but rather to hear the evidence as it is presented and make a decision solely on that evidence. Consequently, the regulation writers emphasized that whoever is chosen as a hearing officer cannot have a personal or professional interest that would affect his or her objectivity.[3]

When my state first began implementing the law, it refused to set up a hearing officer system. We sued; the federal government withheld EHA dollars; and the state created a system in which the commissioner

---

Jason is the name of the youngster whose case allowed us to challenge a hearing officer. Jason's needs were met rather quickly by cooperation between the school district and the state education agency. Nothing in this chapter actually describes Jason's situation.

of education served as hearing officer, with his decisions reviewed by the state board of education. We sued again, and the state removed the state board. We sued again; the state removed the commissioner and initiated a system of appointing several attorneys in the state to hear cases.

That system worked. Both sides had confidence in its impartiality; that, to me, was the key. But the system also had another very important function. The Supreme Court had said in *Rowley* that a court should defer to the findings of a hearing officer.[4] The hearing was basically the trial: Evidence was introduced, witnesses were cross-examined, a record was produced. Whatever happened after that point would always come back to the findings of fact and conclusions of law stated by the hearing officer. Thus, impartiality was key for that reason. If that record was going to be relied upon all the way through judicial appeals, then it was crucial to make sure that the record would be developed fairly.

There is another important reason to protect the integrity of this system. The hearing officer's decisions should form the basis of administrative law in the state. After a period of time and a number of decisions, there should be a good understanding of how the law is developing. If the decisions have been impartial and both sides can respect them, then the developing law should solve a lot of problems.

Congress saw the impartial hearing decisions as giving the state agency valuable information as well. A review of the complaints leading to hearings and of the decisions will reveal if there is some large unsolved problem in the state. Congress required that the hearing officers' decisions be sent to the state advisory committee.[5] That committee, charged with advising the state on unmet needs, could say, for example, "It is obvious that the state needs to develop a policy on extended school year services and that the policy must include the requirements stated in these hearing officer decisions." That is what Congress intended.

One final reason exists for impartial hearings. If the hearing is truly impartial, then each party has an invaluable piece of information: how its case would play before a federal judge. Any litigant should take a deep breath, read the decision objectively, and honestly consider whether an appeal would be productive. If, however, the hearing system is not impartial, the loser will simply say, "Let's get on to the next level," and an important reason for having an administrative level of review would be lost.

I was afraid that the hearing system in our state was about to be compromised. The state education agency had employed an attorney in its Office of General Counsel to handle special education matters. Consequently, we had to interact frequently. He represented the state agency when we had named it as a defendant. He always argued vigorously that the state could not be a defendant because a hearing officer could not exercise jurisdiction over that state agency. He always lost that jurisdictional argument in our cases, but I enjoyed him as an adversary because of his intelligence, humor, and fervor. I also liked him because he had chosen to commit his time to special education law, an area that seems often overlooked by lawyers moving up in the state education agency.

While this individual served in the state education agency he helped formulate and revise state special education policy concerning notice to parents, discipline of students with disabilities, residential placement, educational services to residents of state schools for persons with retardation, interagency agreements between the state education agency and other state agencies serving students with disabilities, and extended school year services.

Some of this attorney's changes were very good, and some were, I felt, awful. We remained friendly foes and, as such, had many private discussions. He often complained about decisions of our state's hearing officers and expressed the wish that he could be the sole hearing officer for the state. After one rather heated exchange between the two of us before the state board of education concerning a rule change, we walked out of the hearing room together, and he informed me that he was in fact going to realize his ambition.

The contracts for employment with hearing officers were handled through our state attorney general's office. I inquired of that office whether this individual was to become the sole hearing officer, and I received rather guarded responses. However, after several conversations, I sensed that the deal was in the works. I told everyone possible that I would have to sue if that happened. If there was any response to my threat, I certainly never detected one.

I took another tack. A hearing officer called me about a case in progress, and I asked if I could pose a rather curious question. As nonprejudicially as I could, I very cautiously asked if that hearing officer had recently had any unusual communication from the state education agency. The reply was "Do you mean have I been fired?" I said yes, and the hearing officer explained that he had been informed that no more cases would be assigned to him. I asked if he knew whether any other hearing officer had received a similar communication, and he did not know. I called a second hearing officer, who replied affirmatively. I called a third, and he replied negatively. It would certainly be ridiculous to file a suit on that basis.

Then the news broke. A colleague returned from an annual meeting of special education directors and stated that the future hearing officer had addressed the group. According to my colleague, he had said that on the last day of that month he would leave the state education agency and on the following day would become the sole hearing officer for the state.

I looked for a case in preparation that would properly raise the issue of impartiality. We filed in Jason's case and were assigned this new hearing officer. In that case we would be raising issues such as notice, extended school year services, and interagency agreements. We would be contesting the very rules and regulations that the new hearing officer had written. The impartiality issue was clearly ripe, and we filed suit.[6]

We told the court of the impartiality requirement, that "a hearing may not be conducted by any person having a personal or professional interest which would conflict with his or her objectivity in the hearing."[7] We listed the issues that we would be raising and contrasted them with the issues that the hearing officer had developed as policy. We pointed out that we would be naming the state education agency as a defendant and that the hearing officer had frequently argued that hearing officers could have no jurisdiction over his former employer. We pointed out that his former colleagues would be witnesses and a former colleague would be defense counsel.

Part of our complaint was that the state education agency did not appropriately inform parents of their right to an impartial hearing; the agency simply stated that the hearing officer could not have a personal or professional connection with the school. We wondered how many parents out there had been assigned this hearing officer and had no way of knowing about the fuller requirements for impartiality.

Our circuit court of appeals had not ruled on this issue, but our "sister circuit," the Eleventh, had heard a similar case. In that case[8] the state used university personnel as hearing officers. Some of the personnel were familiar with special education law because they were part of a panel that had helped develop special education regulations. The court found that "when a university professor has taken an active part in formulating a state policy in the area of special education, it seems entirely plausible that he could become sufficiently personally or professionally invested in the policy that he would find it difficult to reverse or modify it as a due process hearing officer."[9] That court barred the university personnel from serving on *any* case, not just cases involving policies they had developed.

Our circuit court of appeals had ruled on judicial impartiality under another statute,[10] stating that the goal of such statutes was "to create and promote public confidence in the judicial system by avoiding even the appearance of partiality."[11] The court stated that the test for disqualification of a judge should be "if the reasonable man, were he to know all the circumstances, would harbor doubts about the judge's impartiality."[12]

We felt that we had a strong case, and an attorney representing one of the defendants asked to talk. He said, "What are you really after?" As we discussed it, I realized that he was concerned about a revolving-door ethics policy that would prohibit agency employees or elected officials from leaving office and then lobbying or arguing cases before their former administrative or political bodies. A federal judicial ruling in our case could possibly curtail the activities of a legion of lobbyists and lawyers in our state.

I said that, honestly, all I wanted was to have someone take a fresh look at the ability of this hearing officer to be impartial. My client Jason's situation had already been resolved, but I did not want to have to go through this process again and again. I knew I could trust the attorney I was talking to; he said that if I withdrew the case, it would be taken care of.

It was. We now have a system that has all the flaws of any judicial undertaking but that is truly impartial.

## Notes

1. 348 F.Supp. 866 (D.D.C. 1972).
2. Mills, at 880.
3. 34 C.F.R. 300.506.
4. Board of Education v. Rowley, 458 U.S. 176 (1982), at 206.
5. 20 U.S.C. 1415(d). See also 34 C.F.R. 300.508(a)(5).
6. Advocacy, Incorporated and Jason S. v. Kirby, Civ. No. A–86–CA–543 (W.D. TX 1986).
7. 34 C.F.R. 300.507(a)(2).
8. Mayson v. Teague, 749 F.2d 652 (11th Cir. 1984).
9. Mayson, at 659.
10. Health Services Acquisition Corp. v. Liljeberg, 796 F.2d 796 (5th Cir. 1986).
11. Liljeberg, at 800.
12. Liljeberg, at 800.

# Parental Reimbursement

When Steven's case on extended school year services (chapter 7) was successfully concluded, the issue remained of reimbursement for his mother. She had paid the expenses of Steven's summer services herself. The school, seeing those expenses as unauthorized, refused to consider such reimbursements. Similarly, when Sterling's case (chapter 8) was revived on appeal, it was because of an unresolved issue regarding parental reimbursement for extended school day services. In that case, also, the school refused to consider reimbursement.

Both schools took the position held by most school districts at that time—that a parent cannot unilaterally decide on a service, run up a bill, and then ask for reimbursement. How could a school set up an annual budget and stretch its thin resources for all the children it had to serve if one parent could go out and incur an expense not on the budget? Several courts, in fact, had ruled that such unilateral action without notice to the school or approval by the IEP committee meant that the parents waived their rights under the Education of the Handicapped Act (EHA). In Steven's case the district court had refused to allow reimbursement "because Steven was placed in those summer programs unilaterally, without the approval of or consultation with the School District."[1]

The United States Supreme Court clarified this issue just in time for Steven's and Sterling's cases. And Steven's case answered a question left open by the Supreme Court, thus establishing an important additional rule on reimbursement that courts are now following.

A case I had worked on years before as a consulting attorney at the hearing and district court levels had gone through a tortuous procedural history before ending up in the Supreme Court. The persistence of the parent, which I had come to know well, and the dedication of the lead attorney kept it going. The case, *Burlington School Committee v. Department of Education*,[2] concerned a student with a learning disability whose father felt that the child was in an inappropriate program. Seeing the youngster's positive response to private programming during summer breaks in the public school program, the father urged the public school to adopt the successful approach. When it refused, the father unilaterally placed the child in the private facility at his own expense. He then sought a hearing to make the public school reform its program and to be reimbursed for his expenses.

Should parents be expected to stand by and leave their child in a public school program if they think the child is deteriorating? Should Sterling's mother have ignored the risks for her son when she knew of a facility that could not only prevent further harm but also actually help him address his needs? How could Steven's mother face another summer with no programming when she had seen appropriate summer programming keep her child from irreparably losing skills? Many parents across the country must have been considering the same questions. Most, I presume, were unable to act because they assumed that the funding would be their own responsibility.

The Supreme Court in *Burlington* issued a simple ruling. The Court first addressed whether reimbursement was possible under the EHA:

> The first question on which we granted certiorari requires us to decide whether this grant of authority includes the power to order school authorities to reimburse parents for their expenditures on private special education for a child if the court ultimately determines that such placement, rather than a proposed IEP, is proper under the Act. We conclude that the Act authorizes reimbursement.[3]

If reimbursement is permissible, then does unilateral action by parents waive their rights? The Supreme Court answered unequivocally:

> The provision says nothing about financial responsibility, waiver, or parental right to reimbursement at the conclusion of judicial proceedings. Moreover, if the provision is interpreted to cut off parental rights to reimbursement, the principal purpose of the Act will in many cases be defeated in the same way as if reimbursement were never available.[4]

The Supreme Court rule was incredibly clear. A school must reimburse a parent for "expenses that it should have paid all along and would have borne in the first instance had it developed a proper

IEP.["5] The Court specified that this included parents' "expenditures on private special education."[6]

When the *Burlington* decision came down, I was asked to write an analysis of it and entitled the piece "The End of the Take-It-Or-Leave-It IEP." Several schools criticized me for that title, but I hope they understood the message. If a school offers a take-it-or-leave-it approach (e.g., we only offer one session of physical therapy per week; we only offer consultative rather than one-on-one services; we do not offer summer programming; we do not offer extended school day programming), then it is not offering a proper IEP plan.

Development of a proper IEP plan follows all the requirements for individualized decision making. A proper IEP plan might reflect the conclusion that a child does not need extended school year services, but a proper IEP plan cannot be based on a prior decision not to offer such services.

School officials must understand that a proper IEP plan results when all the decisions are made at the IEP meeting. When a school has policies that tie the hands of the IEP committee, that prevent decision making that is *personalized, tailored,* and *specially designed* to meet the *unique needs* of a child (see chapter 3 on the *Rowley* decision), there can be no proper IEP plan.

If parents decide to go outside and purchase private education or related services, they may well be entitled to reimbursement. The question for the court will be "What would a proper IEP plan have prescribed?" If a proper IEP plan for Steven would have included extended school year services, then his mother could be reimbursed. If a proper IEP plan for Sterling would have included extended school day services, then his mother could be reimbursed.

One question, however, went unanswered in *Burlington*. The Supreme Court told us that when the school does it wrong, the parent can be reimbursed. Does that give the parents a blank check? Once there is a flaw in the IEP plan, can a parent purchase any kind of service at any cost? Obviously not, but what standard can we use to judge the appropriateness of parents' expenditures? That question was answered in Steven's case.

The district court had ruled that Steven's mother could not be reimbursed. By the time the case was decided by the Fifth Circuit Court of Appeals, the Supreme Court had issued its *Burlington* decision, which the circuit court had to follow. Now reimbursement was appropriate.

Clearly, the IEP plan of the school district, which had refused to consider individualized summer services, was not "proper." As a result of the district's refusal, Steven's mother had arranged for services over two summers. The first summer she had placed her child at a day care

center, the Learning Tree, which had no expertise in special education and where the program was less than what a school district would
have been required to provide. The following summer, Steven was
placed at Warm Springs Rehabilitation Hospital, where he received
more than one could have imagined in a summer program. The cost
was also more than anyone would expect: $9776.

The school district argued that a proper IEP plan that provided for
extended school year services would not have called for either program. The district seemed to propose, as a standard for reimbursement, that the parent's privately procured services match what the
school should have provided. We argued in our brief that the parent
could not be held to that standard. Parents cannot create programs
to meet their standards as a school district can; they must purchase
what is available.

How, then, do you allow parental choice but not unreasonable expenditures? The Fifth Circuit enunciated in Steven's case the standard
now adopted by other courts:

> In this case, while the district court found that Steven
> was entitled to some sort of continuous, structured sum-
> mer programming, it did not explicitly find that the
> substitute summer placements chosen by Mrs. G. con-
> stituted the specific type of programming necessitated
> by the Act. This distinction, however, need not preclude
> Mrs. G. from receiving *any* reimbursement from the
> school district. The rationale behind *Burlington's* holding
> is that parents who elect to risk shouldering the costs of
> what they perceive to be a more appropriate placement,
> and whose judgment is wholly or in part vindicated by
> the district court, should receive more than an "empty
> victory."
>
> Mrs. G. may be entitled to full reimbursement of her ex-
> penses for the 1981 summer when Steven was enrolled in
> the Learning Tree day care center. Such a program,
> although it might not have been adequate under the
> EAHCA [Education for All Handicapped Children Act],
> was better than no summer program at all. The *Burling-
> ton* rule is not so narrow as to permit reimbursement only
> when the interim placement chosen by the parent is
> found to be the exact proper placement required under
> the Act.
>
> Factors that the court may consider in determining
> whether full or partial reimbursement is in order would

include the existence of other, perhaps more suitable, substitute placements, the effort expended by Mrs. G. in securing alternative placements, and the general cooperative or uncooperative position of the school district itself.[7]

Thus, the court would be balancing three considerations:

1. Were there some suitable services available that the parents passed over for a more expensive one, or did they choose the only alternative available?

2. To judge whether the parents chose among a range of alternatives or took the only one available, how far and wide did they search? Did they take the first thing they found?

3. To judge whether the school district could have helped lessen the cost it is now complaining about, how cooperative was the school in helping the parents find a reasonably priced, suitable alternative?

In Steven's case, the mother searched her entire metropolitan community. The closest alternative she could find was too far for a daily commute, so Steven had to reside at that facility. There were no other alternatives apparent to anyone. The school district was quite uncooperative and left Steven's mother absolutely on her own. Thus, taking those three factors into account, the court ordered full reimbursement. Steven's mother was repaid all her expenses, including the $9776 for the summer program at Warm Springs.

In Sterling's case, the mother had arranged for services after school hours, then on weekends, then during the summers. School district officials said that they would never have considered such extended school day or extended school year programming. Sterling's mother did not really shop around for alternatives. Her previous "shopping" (if that is what you could call her placement of Sterling in the Autistic Treatment Center's day and residential programs, in the hospital program, and in the public school program) had located the remarkable consultant who worked so wonderfully with Sterling. There was virtually nothing else available that she could afford. And the school district seemed to ratify her choice by hiring this individual to be the district's own consultant during school hours.

Finally, how cooperative was the school district in helping Sterling's mother find these extra services? The school district went into court to terminate her parental rights when she suggested that those services were needed. That was perhaps the ultimate definition of uncooperativeness. Sterling's mother received every penny she had spent for the extended day, extended week, and extended year services.

## Notes

1. Alamo Heights Independent School District v. State Board of Education, 790 F.2d 1153 (5th Cir. 1986), at 1160.
2. 471 U.S. 359 (1985).
3. Burlington, at 369.
4. Burlington, at 372.
5. Burlington, at 371.
6. Burlington, at 369.
7. Alamo Heights, note 1, supra, at 1161.

# Attorney Fee Awards

The chilling effect of the Supreme Court decisions in *Smith v. Robinson* and *Tatro*, that attorneys' fees could not be awarded under the Education of the Handicapped Act (EHA), was felt immediately around the country. I had received an attorney fee award in every case I had initiated during the 7-year period from 1977 to 1984, when the Acts had been in effect. We had always invoked the EHA, Section 504 of the Rehabilitation Act, and the Due Process and Equal Protection Clauses of the United States Constitution. Now we were told that the EHA was an exclusive remedy and that no other statutes could be relied on. This meant not only that winning parents could not be reimbursed for attorneys' fees but also that their children would not have the protection of Section 504 or of the Constitution or other laws.

When we began a case, the parents, like any clients talking to an attorney, would ask, "How much is this going to cost?" The answer always had to be "There is no way to tell." I had never started a case that I did not feel I could win, so I was willing to work on a contingency basis (I would be paid by the other side after winning). But I could not afford to do that now, so I had to try to answer the question about cost. However, it was impossible to give such an estimate.

The reason, as seen in Amber's case (chapter 5), was that even after winning conclusively at the circuit court of appeals in 1980, the parents were then dragged back to the district court, where they won again; they were dragged back to the circuit court, where they won again; and, finally, they were dragged to the Supreme Court, where they won 9 to 0 on the substantive issues in the case. It was not up to the parents to stop the case. Because the school district had the resources to keep the case going as long as the courts would hear it (and the school attorneys' bills were being paid at the end of each month), the parents were stuck. There was thus no way to forecast the expense when a parent first asked about legal costs. I would have to answer, "Tell me first whether the school district will drag this out and how many hours I will have to put into the case."

The hours expended in the *Tatro* case, multiplied by a reasonable hourly rate (which was lower in 1978 and rose through 1989, when the case was concluded), produced a fee request of approximately $225,000. Any parent asking, "How much is it going to cost?" who is told, "I don't know, but it might run as high as $225,000," would presumably say, "Forget it." The uncertainty about the amount of the fee, and the difficulty after the *Tatro* decision of recovering it from the other side, would keep parents from contacting lawyers in the first place.

At one school district gathering shortly after the *Tatro* case was decided, I was told that an employee of Amber's school district was asked what the district was going to do. He reportedly replied, "We're thinking about not doing the catheterization. What are they going to do, sue us again?" According to the administrator telling me this story, all the other personnel laughed. That was exactly the chilling effect that was feared around the country: Schools would feel that they had unlimited dollars for their lawyers and now assumed that parents would not be able to afford lawyers of their own.

The outcry in Congress was immediate, and consideration of an amendment to the EHA, which became known as the Handicapped Children's Protection Act, began. The United States Senate quickly considered the bill and passed it. Amber's mother was invited to testify and provided powerful testimony about the impact of not being able to receive attorneys' fees. The Senate Committee Report, which was part of the legislative history of the EHA, noted the wrong done to the Tatro family:

> The testimony by Mary L. Tatro before the Subcommittee on the Handicapped last May portrays a clear example of a school district extending judicial proceedings for more than 5 years in an attempt to force the Tatro family to drop their case due to exorbitant costs of attorneys' fees. The Tatros' legal fees exceeded $200,000. If it were not for the assistance of a public advocacy group willing to take their case, they would have been forced to abandon their daughter Amber's cause and thus give up the right of Amber to attend school and receive a decent education.[1]

But when the House of Representatives considered the bill, the battle lines were really drawn. The American Association of School Administrators and the National Association of School Boards decided to mount an all-out attack. The feeling was that if they could keep this bill from becoming law, and keep parents who prevailed under the EHA from being reimbursed for their attorneys' fees, special educa-tion litigation against school districts could be severely limited.

One lead witness was a school district representative who testified about the amount of attorney fee awards that his school district had been required to pay. Only under questioning from committee members did the representative admit that the district had never paid an attorney fee award in a special education case; rather, it had been paying awards after losing other kinds of cases.

Several facts became apparent. For instance, the bulk of litigation in most school districts was from teachers suing their administration over salary and employment disputes. Similarly, the largest dollar awards in attorneys' fees and damages against school districts were from "regular" students who were injured on school property. After 7 years of litigation under the EHA, schools could not honestly report large awards in special education cases. But what that school district witness (and his supporters in the House committee) wanted was no special education litigation at all.

During the House committee deliberations, a number of amend-ments were introduced that attempted in every way possible to make the Senate version of the bill unworkable. First was an amendment that would not specifically overturn the relevant Supreme Court cases and would not really allow attorneys' fees.

When that was defeated, an amendment was introduced to say that no attorneys' fees would be awarded if none had in fact been incurred. This meant that if a parent had been represented by legal services or by one of the protection and advocacy services set up by Congress through the Developmental Disability Act, attorneys' fees would not have been charged to the parent, and therefore an award would not be possible. Civil rights law in other areas had allowed attorney fee awards without regard to whether fees had actually been charged. Because much of the litigation in the country on special education cases was being conducted by protection and advocacy services (in fact, Amber's family was represented from 1981 to 1989 in part by their state's protection and advocacy service), this amendment would mean that very little would be awarded for attorneys' fees.

When that amendment was defeated, an attempt was made to place a cap on the total amount of attorneys' fees that could be awarded in any given case. The absurdity of this was made clear by Amber's case: How could a lawyer agree to take on a case in which the investment of time and cost was unknown but in which it was clear that, beyond a certain amount, there would be no reimbursement? For example, if a cap were instituted and the parents won their case but were dragged along for 8 more years, as were the Tatros, how could the parents convince their attorney to keep going beyond the point where payment for time and expenses was allowed? The school district attorney, in contrast, would be paid every month; the cap would act either to prevent parents from getting an attorney in the first place or to keep the attorney from continuing until the end. It would be like a poker game in which the school was allowed unlimited opportunities to raise the bet but the parents would have to fold when the bet reached a certain amount. That, of course, is what opponents of the Senate bill wanted to happen.

The next amendment attempted a cap on hours so that only a certain number of attorney hours could be reimbursed in any one case. Again, Amber's case provided the perfect argument against such an amendment. Who knew, when her case was begun, that it would go on for 10 years and involve thousands of hours? What attorney could agree to take a case, not knowing whether he or she could honestly represent the client within the number of hours predetermined by Congress?

Finally, there was an attempt to set a cap on the hourly fee that could be reimbursed. The suggested rate was very low, clearly intended to discourage lawyers from bothering with this area of the law. It was mentioned to the legislators that they had recently approved fees requested by attorneys representing several members of the Nixon and Reagan administrations. Those attorneys had billed at, and were awarded, rates many times higher than the cap that the present amendment would have allowed for special education cases. All of these limiting amendments were defeated.

Both the House and the Senate did anguish over how to allow the reimbursement of reasonable attorneys' fees without allowing a parent's attorney to turn on the meter, drag out the litigation, and run up a huge bill. That specter, however, seemed amusing to attorneys who actually represented parents. To them, the attorneys representing school districts were the ones who turned on the meter, protracted the litigation, billed the client (and were paid) every month, and had an obvious interest in keeping the case going.

The attorneys who represented the school district in Amber's case were paid monthly, whereas those representing the family had to wait 10 years for the case to be concluded and to receive their first penny. So, who benefits more from lengthy proceedings: the school attorney, who is guaranteed to be paid the amount billed each month as long as the case is kept going? Or the parents' attorney, who may receive no award—or receive only a fraction of the expected award—and who must, in any case, wait until the end to receive whatever the award turns out to be?

When the legislation allowing attorneys' fees in the case was finally passed[2] and negotiations began to secure the attorney fee award in the *Tatro* case, I offered to settle the family's claim for exactly what the school district had paid its attorneys up to that point. The reaction was a definite no. It was as if attorneys representing school districts were real professionals who deserved to be paid but an attorney representing a parent was somehow not worth the same compensation. (And, of course, such a discussion about paying the parents' attorney's fees would occur only if the parents had prevailed and were therefore entitled to a fee award. That is, the parents' attorney had to beat the school attorney. In the *Tatro* case, the parents prevailed 9 to 0 at the Supreme Court.)

In another case I handled shortly after this, the school attorney declined to pay the parents any fee because "schools should not have to pay attorneys' fees." I said, "That's right. Schools should not have to pay attorneys' fees. So if you pay back all the fees you have been paid, we will waive our fee, and your district will not have to pay any attorneys' fees." I won't repeat the language from the school's attorney, but my offer was clearly rejected.

The battle raged in Congress for 25 months on how to balance the presumably overcharging and overprotracting parents' attorneys against the school district attorneys, who presumably wanted to wrap up each case as expeditiously as possible. Congress ended up with a fair balance: The parents' fee request would be scrutinized for reasonableness of hours and rates, and the number of hours or the rate could be reduced at the court's discretion unless it was found that the school district had protracted the proceeding.

Scrutiny of the parents' attorney fee request had already occurred in the *Tatro* case, because that was basically the law all along. The district court, in 1981, had cut some of the hours and the rate for the chief attorney involved.[3] The district court was obliged to hear the case again because the parents' attorney had won overwhelmingly at the circuit court level, and that court had ordered the district court to change its opinion. The district court showed some hostility to the winning parents' attorney in its language and the way it chopped the fee. That is precisely the risk a plaintiff's attorney takes. There is no forum, however, for someone to examine the fee of the losing school district's attorney and say it should have been less.

The same scrutiny occurred with regard to costs in the *Tatro* case. The circuit court had ordered the school to reimburse the Tatros for the cost of private schooling during the time Amber was barred from the school district. The district court looked at every way possible to reduce the reimbursement below the actual cost but reluctantly admitted that the full cost had to be awarded.

When the Handicapped Children's Protection Act was finally passed in 1986, it specifically overturned *Smith v. Robinson*[4] and was retroactive to the day before the *Tatro* decision. We could thus collect our full attorneys' fees. When we proceeded for an award of attorneys' fees incurred from 1978 through 1986, the other side challenged the number of hours we had spent on each segment of the case and the hourly rate charged. We sought through discovery proceedings to find exactly what the school attorneys had billed: the number of hours for each segment (the administrative proceedings, the district court the first time, the circuit court appeal the first time, the district court the second time, the circuit court the second time, and the Supreme Court) and the hourly rate charged from 1978 to the present. The school district refused to tell us, or the court, those figures.

We argued to the court that the most logical way to determine whether our hours and rate were fair would be to compare them with what the school attorneys had considered fair to bill their client. But the school attorneys did not want that known; they even hired an "expert" attorney to argue that they need not make such a disclosure. We found it amusing that the school attorneys were willing to run up an even higher bill to avoid revealing how high their original bill had been. But the local newspaper did not find it amusing and asked, through the state Open Records Act, for the information. The school attorneys fought that request as well.

When I put together the fee request for the five attorneys who had worked on the case as it stretched over 8 years, I discovered that the time records of one attorney for 1983 and 1984 had been lost. Pursuant to the procedures of the Fifth Circuit, I reconstructed the hours. I then filed an affidavit proclaiming that these were reconstructed hours and that, if the school district officials wanted to challenge them, they could tell us the amount of hours they had billed for that segment, and the court could compare them. The school district remained silent.

It then became apparent, in 1986, that we would have to keep litigating this 8-year-old case. The Handicapped Children's Protection Act gave us the right to seek fees from both losing parties: the local school district and the state education agency. We met with representatives of the state agency, who said that they felt they did not bear any responsibility for the problem and thus should not have to pay any fees.

Further, representatives of the state attorney general's office told me they thought it would be "fun" to test the constitutionality of such retroactive legislation, speculating that they could "take it all the way back to the Supreme Court." Thus, the parents faced not only a school district willing to keep spending dollars to avoid paying the parents' attorneys, but also a state education agency willing to spend unlimited funds to take the case all the way through the court system again.

We briefed the constitutionality issue thoroughly. While we were waiting for a decision, a case from a neighboring state reached the Fifth Circuit Court of Appeals, which ruled that the Act was constitutional.[5]

We continued offering to settle the case, but there was no interest on the other side. Who is it that has an interest in prolonging these cases? That is one of the matters on which I eagerly testified to Congress when it requested my testimony a year after the Handicapped Children's Protection Act was passed. The legislators were astonished that after they had passed the Act, and specifically mentioned the Tatro family, the case was still being dragged on.

The amount of our requested fees continued to grow because we were entitled to the fees it took to secure our fees. The district court ruled soundly that we were entitled to our fees and told us to bring our affidavits concerning fees up to date. Our fees stretched over 10 years and several attorneys. Curiously, the only items the other side did not attack in our fee petition were the hours that I had expended in the case and my rate at that time of $200 per hour.

It looked as though the case would continue forever when suddenly the other side agreed to a settlement. We were finally able to say, "It's over." The Tatros' original bittersweet victory at the Supreme Court was now replaced with a very sweet victory. I only hope the Tatros can someday know how many thousands of children and families have benefited because they never gave in and never gave up.

The following year a national disability rights group gave its first "Advocate of the Year" award. I sat in the audience and watched proudly as Mary Tatro received the award.

# Notes

1. *Senate Report* 99–112 (1985), pp. 17–18.
2. Handicapped Children's Protection Act, Public Law 99–372, 20 U.S.C. 1415(e)(4), (f).
3. 516 F.Supp. 968 (N.D. TX 1981).
4. 468 U.S. 992 (1984).
5. Fontenot v. Board of Education, 805 F.2d 1222 (5th Cir. 1986).

# Epilogue

The first 15 years of implementation of the Education of the Handicapped Act (EHA) and Section 504 of the Rehabilitation Act focused largely on inputs. Attention was paid to getting notice, timely evaluations, proper persons at the IEP meetings, properly credentialed personnel, and so forth. In 1990, Congress reviewed the EHA (now called the Individuals with Disabilities Education Act, or IDEA) and considered some disturbing facts. The dropout rate for students with disabilities is significantly higher than for other students. The percentage of special education students who go on to postsecondary education is one-fourth the rate of other students. And worst of all, the employment rate for persons with disabilities is much lower than for the general population. The result, then, of 15 years and 10 billion dollars worth of effort is that most students will leave special education and live boring lives at home or in institutions, although they are capable of much more.

Congress shifted the focus in the 1990 amendments to outcomes. They want special education to make a difference. When we focus on that annual IEP plan and lose sight of that year's relationship to the eventual outcome for the student, we lose our goal. Thus, Congress created the new requirement in the IEP process of the "transition plan." Now, at age 16 (or earlier if appropriate) the IEP plan will not only set annual goals, procedures, and so forth, it will also link that year to the student's future.

Congress defined transition services in those 1990 amendments as follows:

> A coordinated set of activities for a student, designed within an outcome-oriented process, which promotes movement from school to post-school activities, including post-secondary education, vocational training, integrated employment (including supported employment),

continuing and adult education, adult services, independent living, or community participation. The coordinated
set of activities shall be based upon the individual student's
needs, taking into account the student's preferences and
interests, and shall include instruction, community experiences, the development of employment and other
post-school adult living objectives, and, when appropriate,
acquisition of daily living skills and functional vocational
evaluation.[1]

This focus on outcomes will take the curriculum in new directions.
Many schools have stuck with commercially available curricula based
on a general developmental notion (i.e., until the student can point
to the red triangle, he or she cannot go to the next step). The result
of that approach has been many years of frustrating instruction, with
students either dropping out or graduating with no real-life skills.
Outcome-focused curricula will take many students out of the classroom, into community based experiences. More students will be
working on-site and learning their reading and mathematics in rela-
tion to their work.

Further, social skills will be a bigger part of the curriculum. Many
schools claim that socialization skills are not a legitimate part of the
curriculum. However, research uniformly shows that the reason individuals with disabilities are not hired, or are fired, is not a lack of
technical skills but a lack of acceptable social behaviors. The first student I caused to be placed in a job setting part-time was sent home
the first afternoon. The vocational counselor told me the job site
supervisor said he "would not put up with a punk like that." When
the transition plan includes an expectation of employment, the job
of education will not be complete until necessary social skills are
added to the technical skills needed.

Congress recognized in these 1990 amendments that some students
lack another ingredient in reaching the outcomes we all wish for. All
of us want our school graduates to be fully included in the life of their
community. But many students with disabilities lack recreation and
leisure skills. One continuing assumption in the IDEA is that education is to prepare individuals with disabilities for life after school ends.
Congress recognized that "students with disabilities have unique
leisure needs which require specialized assessment and education services to allow them to develop, to the maximum extent feasible, fulfill-
ing, independent leisure lifestyles."[2]

Congress thus expects schools "to employ and utilize therapeutic
recreation professionals to evaluate, plan, and administer the recreation component of an individual's education plan." Congress further

stated it expects these "intensive recreation services" to be provided in educational settings with the aim of developing "the skills necessary to participate in other integrated social and community settings." Thus, school is once again the place to teach certain students the skills they need to be fully included in community life—an indispensable outcome for education.

The third focus of Congress in the 1990 amendments was the integration of students with disabilities into the life of the school. If it makes sense to have transition plans that will place students successfully in the larger community, and to teach recreation skills to get our graduates into the social life of the community, then it makes sense to concentrate on how those students are doing while they are still in school. Are they learning those vital socialization skills and moving toward more integrated environments? Or are they in segregated, harmful environments that teach them dependency and steer them away from any chance of eventually merging into their community?

Congress has ordered a study to find out why some schools segregate the very type of students that other schools are able to integrate. Another study will identify specific practices having the potential to integrate children with disabilities with children who are not disabled. Congress clearly wants an end to the segregation during school years that defeats the purpose of education and will lead to segregation for the rest of those individuals' lives.

Thus, the next few years will be challenging. Schools will be challenged to actually produce results. Employers will be challenged to end discriminatory practices and make reasonable accommodations to employ those successful special education graduates. And all of us, particularly those exposed to students with disabilities as our classmates, will be challenged to include citizens with disabilities in every aspect of our community lives. If that is done, then special education will truly have accomplished Congress's goals.

## Notes

1. 20 U.S.C. 1401 (19).
2. This and subsequent quotations are from *House Report* 101–544 (1990), p. 9.

# Index

115

# About the Author

Reed Martin is an attorney, consultant, and author on disability law. He has served as legislative aide to United States Senator Ralph Yarborough, who chaired the Senate Subcommittee on Education and Health, and has been recognized as a national leader in special education since the publication of *Educating Handicapped Children: The Legal Mandate* (Research Press, 1978). Martin has represented over 3000 clients under the Education of the Handicapped Act/Individuals with Disabilities Education Act and Section 504 of the Rehabilitation Act, ranging from IEP meetings through cases heard before the United States Supreme Court. He has consulted with state and local education agencies and consumer organizations in 48 states and has conducted over 250 day-long conferences on disability law in 35 states. Martin has been an adjunct professor at the University of Houston Graduate School of Psychology, teaching law and psychology. He has produced a series of 12 videotaped lectures, *Legal Challenges in Special Education*, and three audiotapes, *Parents in the Special Education Process*, distributed by Carle Center for Health Law and Ethics, Urbana, Illinois. He has written and edited 11 publications of cases and materials on disability law issues, the latest of which is *Special Education Law: Changes for the Nineties* (Carle Center, 1991). His next book, forthcoming from LRP Publications, is *Special Education Law Practice and Procedure Manual*.